A Book for a Sixpence

A BOOK FOR A SIXPENCE,

The Circulating Library in America

by David Kaser

· BETA PHI MU ·

1980

Beta Phi Mu Chapbook Number Fourteen
Published by Beta Phi Mu, Pittsburgh, Pennsylvania
Copyright © Beta Phi Mu, 1980

Library of Congress Cataloging in Publication Data
Kaser, David, 1924-
    A book for a sixpence.

    (Chapbook—Beta Phi Mu; no. 14)
    Bibliography: p.
    Includes index.
        1.   Libraries, Rental—United States—History.
    2.   Libraries—United States—History—18th century.
    3.   Libraries—United States—History—19th century.
    I.   Title.   II.   Series: Beta Phi Mu. Chapbook;
    no. 14.
    Z675.R4K37   027'.3   79-4298
    ISBN 0-910230-14-5

This book is printed on acid-free paper in order to
extend its permanence and durability.

TO KATHI
My favorite since 1963

Contents

LIST OF TABLES

LIST OF ILLUSTRATIONS

Foreword

This is the fourteenth in a series of Beta Phi Mu Chapbooks that began publication a quarter of a century ago with the aim of contributing to the literature of books and libraries, and also of advancing the art of book design. Discussions of bibliography, fine binding, book design, librarians, and a single library have previously appeared in the series, but this is the first chapbook to deal with so broad a library phenomenon as the circulating library in America.

David Kaser, author of this absorbing study, began his career as a librarian at Ball State University in 1952, the year that the first Beta Phi Mu chapbook was being prepared for publication. Since that time he has served at the University of Michigan and Washington University, as Director of the Vanderbilt University (Joint) Libraries, Director of Libraries at Cornell University, Professor of Library Science at Peabody College, and since 1973 has been a Professor in the Graduate Library School at Indiana University. During his career, Dr. Kaser has been President of the Association of College and Research Libraries and was International President of Beta Phi Mu during 1975-1976. He also has edited three library journals, including *College and Research Libraries*, 1962-1969. In addition to numerous professional papers, he has published eight books previous to this one, most of them concerned with printing, books, and libraries.

The designer for *A Book for a Sixpence; The Circulating Library in America* is Bruce Campbell of Princeton University Press. A graduate in graphic design from Indiana University, he has designed books for Princeton during the past six years, winning awards at the Fifty Books of the Year Show, the American Association of University Presses Book Show, and the Philadelphia Book Show. In pursuit of his hobby of printing, Mr. Campbell has produced three limited edition books which he illustrated, printed, and bound.

D. B.

Preface

There has been much discussion in the United States in recent years about charging fees for library services, especially when those services are rendered for profit as commercial enterprises. That discussion has treated commercial libraries as though they came upon the scene only recently, but such is not the case. Profit-oriented library services have been in operation in America for well over two centuries and have made a significant impact upon the social and cultural fabric of the nation.

The literature concerning commercial libraries in America has been very scanty. Shera devoted twenty-eight pages to a review of their role in New England business and literary life before 1850, and Moore prepared a masters thesis chronicling their existence in the Southeast before 1840. Beyond those two pieces, however, there have been only two or three brief papers and nothing more. Library historians have almost completely ignored them, and social and literary historians have mentioned them only in passing. It is to repair that deficiency somewhat that I have prepared this slender monograph. In it I have attempted to bring together some of the more salient events and facts in the matter; to sketch them into the contemporary panorama of American literary, cultural, and social development; and to assess the effect and significance of these past profit-oriented library services in American life.

I have benefitted greatly from the assistance of three people in the preparation of this work. Professor C. Haynes McMullen of the University of North Carolina made his extensive files on early American libraries freely available to me. Ms. Karin Donahue of Indianapolis worked with me as research assistant. And my wife Jane, as she has done so often in the past, put in yeoman duty at several points throughout the project. I am exceedingly grateful for their good help.

I must also express my appreciation for the hospitality and services extended to me so generously by the following institutions: Maryland Historical Society, Library of Congress, Boston Public Library, Historical Society of Pennsylvania, Library Company of Philadelphia, New York Public Library, Massachusetts Historical Society, Harvard University Library, Maine Historical Society, Essex Institute, American Antiquarian Society, Detroit Public Library, Rhode Island Historical Society, Brown University Library, John Carter Brown Library, Boston Athenaeum, Washington County, Md., Public Library, and Indiana University Library. I am also indebted to Indiana University for granting me a sabbatical leave, during which most of the work on this volume was accomplished.

Bloomington, Indiana   D. K.
December 20, 1977

A Book for a Sixpence

Chapter One
The Setting: Culture in the Colonies

It was William Rind, as far as can be determined today, who first sensed that he could perhaps turn a profit by lending books out of his Annapolis bookstore in return for an annual subscription fee. That was in 1762. Regrettably for him, his experiment with the scheme appears to have failed, for he abandoned it a few months later. The reasons for its failure are not clear. The idea itself must have been a good one, because hundreds upon hundreds of similar institutions did bring profits to their proprietors during subsequent decades. Perhaps Rind was in the wrong location; maybe he attempted to purvey the wrong books; maybe he was a bit ahead of his time; or perhaps he was simply one of those hapless individuals who was destined to fail in any circumstance. Whatever the reason for his failure, however, Rind established the first of a new kind of institution in America, a kind of institution that was to become a major source of reading to the inhabitants of the New World.

What was the social need that Rind had set out to fill with his commercial library venture, or rather his "circulating library" as such establishments soon came uniformly to be called? Did he perceive there to be in that period of colonial life a shortage of reading material and a superabundance of reading time, or of reading motivation? Were the wrong kinds of reading matter being made available through the conventional channels of literature distribution, or were segments of the population languishing unserved by those channels? Where did Rind get the idea of attempting to operate a library for

(3)

profit? How much originality was there in the concept? Discussion of these questions will provide a setting wherein the history of the phenomenon of America's "circulating libraries" can be most clearly viewed.

Culture and Reading

Life in tidewater America in the middle of the eighteenth century was in many ways a good life. The rugged hardships and deprivations faced by the first immigrants were by now things of the past. Trails and fords had given way to roads and bridges, forests had long since been cleared and planted, and the first rude cabins had been replaced by well-carpentered houses.

It was with good reason a period of economic optimism. Manufacturing was on the rise, and commerce of all kinds was brisk. Population in the Colonies more than quadrupled during the first half of the eighteenth century, and the extensive natural resources of the region were being tapped increasingly. Mercantile opportunities seemed boundless. Rum, sugar, molasses, slaves, tobacco, and iron provided cargo for the expanding fleets of privateers sailing from the thriving ports. Good markets meant full employment for day laborers and journeymen in all trades, and the need for apprentices seemed never to be filled. Yeoman farmers were prospering in the north, as were planters in the south. Shipbuilders, whalers and fishermen, trappers, and land speculators were doing well.

Two conditions—the availability of money and of leisure time—brought about a vigorous growth in cultural activities. Covetous always of the more gracious elements of the Old World life which they had departed, the Colonists seized promptly any new opportunities to add manifestations of culture to their daily existence.

Schools came increasingly to be established, and

(4)

where schools were not yet available (and even sometimes where they were) tutors came increasingly to be retained. There were already four good colleges in the Colonies by midcentury, and two more would be founded in the next five years. Literacy in the Colonies was already high, approaching by some estimates ninety percent in New England and the Middle Atlantic regions.

Interest in art, music, and the theater increased daily. More and more families required portraits to grace the mantels of their more sophisticated homes, providing livelihood for ever-larger numbers of painters, some of whom occasionally also applied their skill to works more imaginative. Painters James Claypoole and John Greenwood had been born in 1720 and 1728 respectively; both John Singleton Copley and Benjamin West were born in 1738.

The first public concert of record in the Colonies was held in Boston in 1729, and others followed quickly. Spinets and harpsichords came increasingly to be found among household furnishings, and sheet music could often be bought from stationers and booksellers, especially in the larger cities. Dancing masters, writing teachers, and fencing instructors published their cards in the many gazettes and newsletters.

The theater was late blooming in the Colonies, in part because of religious opposition, but it had nonetheless begun to establish itself as a cultural force by the middle of the eighteenth century. The first recorded stage performance by professional actors in America took place in Charleston in 1703, and by 1750 professional companies or amateur performances could be seen in a number of cities, although the first American play actually produced before an audience, Godfrey's *Prince of Parthia*, was not written until 1763. Even where there was no drama, there was sometimes spectacle. Circuses

(5)

did not become part of the American scene until later in the century, but animal acts, jugglers, and oddities came and went bringing small elements of entertainment into the lives of the people. Such frivolities, of course, often met with stern-eyed disapproval from the town fathers as working against the morals and decorum of the community.

Reading, among all cultural activities, enjoyed a favored status in the Colonies. To be sure, books could corrupt, and this fact elicited occasional cautions concerning them. William Penn warned darkly against too much reading, although he himself owned a fine library. Rather than suppress reading entirely, however, it behooved communities to control through the unofficial but effective censorship of social disapprobation the kinds of literature available to their inhabitants.

Reading was viewed as more than a cultural pastime; it was also a requisite tool for life. From the earliest Colonial days, reading had been almost necessary for survival itself. The Bible was as essential a guide to the Kingdom of Heaven as mariners' charts were to the vast Atlantic. Theological books were as essential for the curing of lonesome souls, as were nostrums and recipes for the curing of physical ailments. Books on planting and husbandry, military science, law, and history were needed from the beginning for clawing often precarious existences out of the hostile land, and as a result such volumes competed successfully for the limited cargo space of the earliest vessels bringing immigrants to the New World.

Here, however, as is inexorably true everywhere, a few books were not enough, and soon those whose lot it was to provide leadership to their communities were importing volumes of more varied contents. Elder William Brewster of the Colony of Plymouth left a library of almost 400 volumes at his death in 1644, including works by Bacon, Raleigh, Wither, Hakluyt, and Machiavelli. Governor John Winthrop, Jr. of Connecticut, in the latter half of the seventeenth century, developed an extensive library so diverse as to include both scientific treatises and the works of Pascal and Ronsard. The Mathers and the Rev. Thomas Prince owned large and learned libraries in New England in the first half of the eighteenth century, as did also John Logan and Benjamin Franklin in Pennsylvania and William Byrd in Virginia.

Such universal reading interests as these great private collections attest, however, did not generally bestir the wider populace until the period from 1700 to 1750. Whereas the reading of most Colonists in the seventeenth century had concerned the salvation of the soul and the survival of the body in that order, a much broader range of common reading interests manifested itself in the eighteenth century. Social satire became popular in England with the appearance of the *Tatler* and *Spectator* between 1709 and 1712, and the new genre was quick to find readers in America as well. The Great Awakening of the 1730s revitalized the religious interests of American readers and contributed to a new intellectual ferment among them. By mid-century political concerns were raising their heads, prompting the Colonists to study the gazettes and pamphlets for news and views on the burning issues of the times. But probably of paramount importance to the present study was the appearance in England in 1740 of the first modern novel in the English language—Richardson's *Pamela, or Virtue Rewarded*.

After *Pamela* Richardson produced also *Clarissa Harlowe*, much too long in the original for the popular market but widely available in abridgement, and *Sir Charles Grandison* before retiring from writing in 1753. He had, however, performed a remarkable feat with these three epistolary tales by developing for the first time the emotions and experiences of everyday fictional characters drawn from the humbler levels of English life in a manner that could appeal to a wide spectrum of the growing middle class. Moreover, they dealt with forbidden and titillating themes of seduction and rape, although in a most proper manner with virtue inevitably defended even unto death. They veritably reeked of moral and religious didacticism, as Pamela and Clarissa contemplated their sorry fates and Sir Charles pondered his bounden duty. Their popularity, especially of the first two titles, exceeded anything of the kind to that point in the history of American reading, pointed to a new market for booksellers, and paved the way for a future reading craze that could hardly have been imagined at the time.

Also, however, Richardson's success caused a new kind of unease among those who would guard the minds of readers against unwholesome literature, because his many imitators seldom provided the same immediate practical application of morality. Whereas those who were wont to censor had previously to exercise themselves solely about religious heresy and political heterodoxy, they had now to be concerned also with books that might inflame the ruder and less controllable passions of unwary readers and bring about the moral disintegration of society. Here indeed was a new enemy, one which in the minds of some has not yet been wholly vanquished.

In summary then, reading in America by 1750 could be legitimately pursued to a number of ends. It could buttress religious conviction, provide elements of culture, reveal practical solutions to work-a-day problems, support educational purposes, stimulate political debate, and mirror the inscrutable caprice of fickle society. It could also, however, transport the reader to the fictional world of make-believe, a purpose not wholly accepted by the Colonial psyche as a valid use either of books or of the human mind.

The Availability of Books

There were printers aplenty in the eighteenth-century Colonies to provide the wherewithal for American readers. By the time Rind tried his ill-starred scheme of circulating books, there were printing offices in all thirteen Colonies, producing in total an estimated one thousand titles annually. These products were not all books, of course. Many were broadsides, ephemera, pamphlets, chapbooks, and other slight publications. There were also sermons and tracts, university documents, newspapers and other periodicals, official prints of towns and Colonies, and the ubiquitous almanacs that comprised staple items for printers everywhere well into the next century.

But *books* were also being printed—books by whatever definition one chooses to use. As far as can be told from the record, books on religion were the most numerous, although some scholars, apparently with little reason, question whether or not the record can indeed be trusted on this matter. There were ample books too regarding political issues. Broader philosophical works were also being produced on Colonial presses, as were occasional scientific and technical treatises. Works of the imagination, however, were notably absent from the lists of American imprints of this period.

Works of the imagination could certainly be got by most American readers who wished them through the brisk retail trade in imported books which had long been carried on in the major towns. Although most printing offices trafficked also in retail books (along with stationery, binding, sundries, and even sometimes materia medica) well into the nineteenth century, book-selling itself had already by 1750 become an extensive trade in the larger mercantile centers. It is recorded that the great fire in Boston in 1711 wiped out some thirty bookstores[1] in the vicinity of the Town House, as well as decimating Boston's first public library collection, which was housed in that building. There were fewer booksellers in New York, but one visitor to that city reported calling at "a Number of print-Shops and Booksellers" in 1760.[2] Philadelphia enjoyed a vigorous booktrade in the first half of the eighteenth century, boasting at least six bookstores by 1750, of which Benjamin Franklin's well-stocked shelves reportedly offered the greatest variety. Book auctions, or "vendues" as they were more frequently called, were held at the coffeehouses, and newspapers everywhere advertised books for sale by other merchants.

Wright has observed that these advertisements "indicate a steady market for contemporary English publications and do not suggest that the cultural lag was longer than the time for books to reach the colonies after publication in England."[3] It is indeed true that English books were available promptly in America and that works of the imagination were fully represented among the titles imported. One gentleman in attendance at a Boston book auction in 1744 reported that "the books that sold best . . . were *Pamela, Anti-Pamela, The Fortunate Maid,* Ovid's *Art of Love,* and *The Marrow of Modern Divinity.*"[4] Such being the case, it is to be wondered at that Colonial printers, who were for the most part very responsive to the public whimsy in their selection of titles to be printed, had to that time so studiously avoided the publication of imaginative works. Almost uniformly, it seems, such books prior to mid-century had to be imported to be read. In noting this phenomenon, Wroth avers simply that "it was more economical at this time to procure works of European *belles lettres* in foreign editions than to attempt their republication in this country."[5] Perhaps, but the issue could probably benefit from further investigation.

The newspaper was by 1750 securely ensconced as a prime source of reading matter for the American Colonist. Uniquely American in origin, the newspaper has always enjoyed favored status among Anglo-Saxon readers. It was whilom Boston bookseller, printer, and coffeehouse proprietor Benjamin Harris who first conceived the idea of issuing a periodical news-sheet. On September 25, 1690 he published the first issue of his *Publick Occurrences Both Forreign and Domestick*, but it was suppressed after the single exemplar, and it was not until fourteen years later that a longer-lived newspaper, *The Boston News-Letter*, began publication. Thereafter the genre became a staple ingredient in the American reading diet. By 1730 there were seven papers being published, and thereafter the number rose rapidly as the Colonists found themselves engrossed increasingly in political affairs wherein currency of information and opinion was of growing importance. By the time of William Rind's book-lending experiment, fully fifty-one weekly newspapers had been established in the Colonies. Together with the twelve American magazines that had sprung up during the two previous decades, newspapers were widely read and had become highly influential as molders and shapers of American thought.

Alternatives to Book Ownership

Alternatives to book ownership were also available to some American readers by this time. Merchants and others in the larger cities had only to repair to the local coffeehouse to read the current newspapers and periodicals. It is easy today to overlook the importance of the coffeehouses as the communication centers of the Colonial towns.[6] They served as a kind of prototype stock exchange, where commercial transactions were often concluded, records of buyers and sellers were maintained, and "prices-current" from other communities were kept at hand. They were also often hostelries with livery facilities, and the proprietor was usually the local postmaster, all of which meant that intelligences from elsewhere arrived first in a community at the coffeehouse. Very often a bookselling establishment was operated in the coffeehouse, and inevitably copies of newspapers from near and far were available to be read by customers. Thus Whitehall's Coffee-House in New York could advertise in 1762 that it received "all the public prints [of England] as soon as possible, and there will be a weekly supply of New York, Boston, and other American papers as well." The same could be claimed by Philadelphia's London Coffee House, which was operated by printer William Bradford III, and by similar establishments in the other towns. Coffeehouse patrons in effect rented access to newspapers and journals (and an occasional few books) with the price of their cup of coffee or mug of ale.

Another alternative to book ownership in some locations by this time was the use of libraries, of which there were then a few. It should be noted that most libraries in this and the subsequent period were book collections only; few had any reading facilities attached to them. The libraries in existence in America in 1762 were primarily of three types. First were the libraries in the half-dozen colleges; they will not be discussed here because they were not generally accessible to the public. Second, there were the book collections which were in one way or another viewed as public property. Boston had maintained a public library of sorts for more than a century, and a public library act had been passed in

South Carolina in 1700 governing use of a book collection in Charleston. Annapolis itself, William Rind's residence, had long maintained a library deposited there for public use in 1696 by the English divine Rev. Thomas Bray.[7] All told, however, it appears unlikely that the number of community-owned libraries in existence in 1762 exceeded ten or a dozen.

Third were the so-called "social libraries," book collections jointly acquired and owned for the mutual benefit of individuals who clubbed together for this specific purpose. The first such institution in America was also the most successful. The Library Company of Philadelphia, established by Benjamin Franklin in 1731, thrives today, still supported largely by the subscription fees of its members. The pattern had much to offer to Colonists interested in wide reading at minimal cost, and such proprietary or associational libraries soon became quite popular. Shera identifies fully sixteen social libraries as having been established in New England alone before 1760,[8] and by the time of the Revolution the number in all of the Colonies is believed to have approached seventy. Subscription fees were quite low in comparison to the extent of reading matter thus made available, and many Colonists availed themselves of this attractive alternative to the individual purchase of books.

Lending Books for Profit

Lending books for profit was already a very old idea by 1762. William Rind was certainly not the first person ever to rent his books to others. Diogenes Laertius stated that it was possible in Athens to consult the works of Plato for a fee.[9] An extensive rental traffic in books was carried on by the stationers of Paris in the fourteenth century,[10] and there are several references to the lending of books for profit in London during the decade of the Restoration.[11] At the end of Webster and Rowley's *The Thracian Wonder,* published in 1661, the printer advertised that he had a stock of ". . . Histories, Romances, or Poetry, which are to be sold, or read for reasonable considerations." Other scattered mentions of book rental in England can be found dating from the subsequent half century. Indeed the whole concept of booksellers renting books to those unable or indisposed to purchase them is entirely too logical to suppose that there was ever a time when it did not go on somewhere.

Allan Ramsay of Edinburgh is usually credited with having first formally developed a collection of novels and romances which he would lend for a fee. He charged a penny a night. That was in 1725. Within the following two decades commercial libraries had found their way to London where the Rev. Samuel Fancourt, a dissenting minister, is reported to have coined the term "circulating library" in 1742.[12] Considering its unspecificity, this term held up remarkably well throughout their great popularity over the subsequent 150 years as referring solely to institutions lending books for profit.

The reasons for the phenomenal success of circulating libraries in England seem to have been largely the same as those in America—a growing middle class with leisure to read, and the coming of age of the novel. In his social history of British popular reading, Altick describes the development as follows:

> . . . important to the growth of the mass reading audience were the commercial libraries that dispensed fiction and other "light literature." While it may have been only a coincidence that a few obscure book and pamphlet vendors were experimenting with the lending of their wares at the very time of the *Pamela* craze, the circulating library was destined

shortly to complete the triangle whose other legs were the expanded middle-class audience and the new fascination of the novel. As the fiction-reading habit spread, circulating libraries sprang up in London, the watering places, the provincial towns, and even in small villages.[13]

Some 365 circulating libraries have been identified as operating at one time or another in Britain, with the vast majority of them flourishing between the mid-eighteenth and the mid-nineteenth centuries.[14]

Fully 53 of these English circulating libraries were in existence prior to 1762 when William Rind first opened his lending operation in Annapolis. They also existed elsewhere in Europe by that time. There was a circulating library in Berlin as early as 1704, and they had come early into existence also in France, Switzerland, and perhaps elsewhere.[15] Rind could therefore have come across his book-rental scheme in any of a number of places. Considering the fact that several other American booksellers followed Rind's lead within only a few months, it appears that the concept was rather generally known in the Colonial booktrade by the early 1760s, but simply not tried prior to that time. Rind certainly claimed no originality for the scheme; in his first announcement he referred to it rather as being "quite new in this Part of the World."[16] Again, however, since the plan is so sensible, it must be allowed that it may actually have been utilized somewhere in America prior to 1762 but that documentation no longer exists. Such, however, seems unlikely.

James Parker, printer of New York, had come very close to operating a library for profit between 1745 and 1747, but technically the books he hired out were not his own.[17] They were rather the property of the Corporation of New York, comprising since 1730 one of the early "public" libraries aforementioned. Languishing largely unused for a period of time, these volumes caught Parker's attention, and in 1745 he proposed to the City Council that he be allowed to assume charge of the books and to circulate them to the residents of the city. He would print a catalogue of the titles in the collection, keep the books in good repair, replace lost copies, open the library for a designated two hours weekly, and rent volumes out for sixpence a week, which would be his only recompense. Equal access to all was not to be part of his plan; he rather proposed that members of the Common Council, which was to decide the fate of his petition, would "be Entituled to the Loan of any Book Gratis And be preferred before all other hirers." Whether in anticipation of their preferential treatment or out of concern for the past desuetude of the library, members of the Council acceded to Parker's representations and delivered custody of the library to him.

Occasional notices in Parker's newspaper, *The New-York Weekly Post-Boy*, indicate his efforts to treat his responsibilities conscientiously. He did issue gratis on June 16, 1746 a catalogue of the books in the collection, and he advertised from time to time for the return of volumes kept overlong by their borrowers. He dropped the price to 4½ d. per week in order to stimulate circulation, and he dutifully attended "said Library Room, every Tuesday at 4 o'Clock in the afternoon" to let out and receive the return of books. When cold weather rendered the library room uncomfortable in the winter of 1746/47, he announced his willingness, if given a day's notice, to fetch particular titles from it for delivery to patrons at his printing office instead. Following 1747, however, there is no further mention of Parker's work with the library, and it is not known how long his relationship to it continued.

Parker probably found his appointment as library

keeper to be profitable. He was the business partner of Benjamin Franklin at the time, and Franklin had had as much experience with libraries as anyone in America. Franklin himself reported having rented books from a bookseller during his stay in London in 1725.[18] He had been the founder of the Library Company of Philadelphia in 1731 and had printed the first catalogue of that collection in 1741, so it may be assumed that he apprised his partner fully of the costs and benefits of performing these several steps in the contemporary practice of librarianship. Since Parker's services and fees were very similar to those of later successful commercial libraries, except that he had neither to put up the requisite capital for establishment of the original collection nor to provide and maintain housing for the operation, it is difficult to see how he could have lost money in the venture. Although interesting as a precursor to the true "circulating library" in America, however, these uniquenesses in Parker's operation place it outside the construct of the present study.

Summary

Cultural activities had begun to come into their own by 1762, with reading the most widely accepted. The motivation to read was strong in the areas of religion, current events and politics, practical arts, and *belles-lettres*. A well-established printing industry was available to meet all literature needs save the last, which was being met rather by importation. Persons wishing to read without purchasing could often gain temporary access to current materials in the coffeehouses and to book collections through publicly-owned or social libraries. The lending of books for profit was already widespread in England and elsewhere by 1762, and at least one experimental venture in America had approached the kind of circulating library being discussed

(17)

here before William Rind established his operation in Annapolis.

REFERENCES

1. George E. Littlefield, *Early Boston Booksellers, 1642-1711* (Boston: Club of Odd Volumes, 1900), p. 13.
2. Quoted in Carl and Jessica Bridenbaugh, *Rebels and Gentlemen* (N.Y.: Reynal & Hitchcock, 1942), p. 97.
3. Louis B. Wright, *Cultural Life of the American Colonies* (New York: Harper & Row, 1957), p. 153.
4. Alexander Hamilton, *Gentleman's Progress: The Itinerarium of Dr. Alexander Hamilton, 1744* (Chapel Hill: University of North Carolina Press, 1948), p. 112.
5. Lawrence C. Wroth, *The Colonial Printer* (Charlottesville: University Press of Virginia, 1964), p. 223.
6. David Kaser, "Coffee House to Stock Exchange: A Natural History of the Reading Room," *Milestones to the Present; Papers from Library History Seminar V* (Syracuse: Gaylord Professional Publications, 1978), pp. 238-54.
7. Charles T. Laugher, *Thomas Bray's Grand Design* (Chicago: American Library Association, 1973), p. 35.
8. Jesse H. Shera, *Foundations of the Public Library* (Chicago: University of Chicago Press, 1949), p. 55.
9. H. L. Pinner, *The World of Books in Classical Antiquity* (Leiden: Sijthoff, 1958), p. 46.
10. George H. Putnam, *Books and Their Makers during the Middle Ages*, 2 vols. (N.Y.: Hillary House, 1962), 1: 204.
11. Devendra P. Varma, *The Evergreen Tree of Diabolical Knowledge* (Washington: Consortium Press, 1972), p. 22.
12. Thomas Kelly, *Early Public Libraries* (London: The Library Association, 1966), pp. 144-45.
13. Richard D. Altick, *The English Common Reader* (Chicago: University of Chicago Press, 1957), pp. 61-62.
14. Varma, *The Evergreen Tree*, pp. 145-92.
15. Ibid., p. xv.
16. *Maryland Gazette*, September 2, 1762.
17. Austin B. Keep, *History of the New York Society Library* (New York: DeVinne Press, 1908), pp. 72-76.
18. *Autobiography*, ed. L. W. Labaree (New Haven: Yale University Press, 1964), p. 97.

Chapter Two
The Beginnings to the Revolution

William Rind of Annapolis

Thus the reputation for being the first person in America to establish a library to be operated for profit falls upon William Rind. Trained as an apprentice to Annapolis printer Jonas Green, Rind had later joined Green as a partner in 1758 to publish the *Maryland Gazette*. From that time forward Rind also operated a small bookstore in his home on West Street, "where the late Mrs. M'Leod formerly kept Tavern."[1]

It was from this address that, on September 2, 1762, Rind proposed his circulating library scheme to the public. The purpose of his library, as he saw it, was a democratizing one: to make available to persons of moderate means the sources of knowledge previously obtainable solely by the wealthy. His proposal, which he published in the *Maryland Gazette*, read in part as follows:

> Among the many Obstacles to literary Acquirements, which the Youth of this Country are liable to, the Want of Books proper to their Instruction, is justly esteemed one of the greatest. The furnishing of a competent Library, for any tolerable Advancement in Letters, requires a Fortune which few people in this Part of the World are Masters of, whence it comes to pass, that many a fine Genius languishes and dies in Obscurity. The Purpose therefore of this Plan, which is to open and extend the Fountains of Knowledge, which are at present shut against all but Men of affluent Fortunes, it is hoped, will meet with the Countenance and Patronage of every Friend to his Country.

Very specifically Rind offered to grant the right to use his library for one year to anyone in Maryland who would pay a subscription fee of Twenty-seven Shillings. Two books could be borrowed at a time, and they could be exchanged at will. Residents of Annapolis and environs could keep folios for periods of up to a month, quartos up to three weeks, and octavos or smaller books for up to one week; but subscribers living farther than thirty miles away could keep books two weeks longer. Lost, unreturned, or damaged books were to be paid for by the patron. Subscribers were not to allow others to read books which they themselves had borrowed.

This earliest known circulating library in America is reported to have been quite slight comprising only about 150 titles, of which approximately one half were English literature, classics, or language. Richardson's *Pamela* was there, as was also his *Clarissa Harlowe*. Fielding was represented by *Tom Jones, Amelia*, and *Joseph Andrews*. Other titles present included Defoe's *Robinson Crusoe*, Montesquieu's *Spirit of Laws*, Voltaire's *Letters on the English Nation*, Fénelon's *Telemachus*, Hanmer's *Shakespeare*, Johnson's *Rambler*, Milton's *Paradise Lost* and *Paradise Regained*, Thompson's *Seasons*, Swift's and Pope's *Works*, and Young's *Night Thoughts*.[2] All in all, it was a well-selected collection of the kinds of books then being read.

Rind's observation that good literature was already available to the wealthy was supported in a letter he received from a prosperous tobacco factor on Maryland's Eastern Shore only three weeks after his prospectus was published. "There is scarce any book in your present Catalogue," he wrote, "that I have not either read or have now by me."[3] Indeed the limited extent of his collection may well have been a key impediment to its success as a profit-bearing venture, although Rind made efforts to broaden his holdings.

He had received "a large shipment" of books from London only days prior to announcing his library, and another invoice of books was dispatched to him from England within two months thereafter. Among titles added were Smollett's *Peregrine Pickle* and Johnstone's allegorical novel *Chrysal*, the plays of Thomas Otway and sometime poet laureate Colley Cibber, Anson's and Charlevoix's travels, theological works of Burnet, Robertson's *History of Scotland*, and such practical works as *The Universal Letter Writer*.[4]

Rind also sought counsel from the public as to how he might render his library more useful, and as usual in such cases the advice he received was often contradictory. Some urged him to expand his collection so as to offer a greater variety of fare; others recommended he restrict his operation closer to Annapolis. Within four months Rind had come to agree that communication throughout Maryland was not yet adequately developed to allow him effectively to serve subscribers flung far throughout the province, and he restricted his service thereafter to persons residing within thirty miles of Annapolis. This restriction probably curtailed his patronage but little because it may be assumed that he had received only limited response from potential subscribers beyond that distance anyway. At the same time he made several modest adjustments in his proposal. Thereafter he would allow only one book to be borrowed at a time. He lowered his subscription rate to One Guinea per year, and he also more than doubled the lengths of the circulation periods for the different size books in his collection.[5] He also indicated his intention to publish a catalogue of his holdings, but it is doubtful that such a catalogue ever appeared.[6]

On February 10 Rind announced to "those Gentlemen and Ladies who have subscribed to his Circulating Library [that] . . . it is now open." The particular wording of this announcement is important for two reasons. First, it makes clear that from the start America's first commercial lending library was intended to serve ladies as well as gentlemen; women were to make up a large share of the readership of such institutions throughout the century and more of their existence. Second, Rind called his enterprise a "Circulating Library", a term which continued to be used almost exclusively for this kind of commercial venture for as long as it was part of the American cultural scene.

Rind, however, was apprehensive from the start that, as he phrased it, his library "is not likely to meet with the Success I expected",[7] and his pessimism proved to be warranted. Within a very few months of operation it was clear to him that public response to his scheme was inadequate to enable him long to continue. He made some effort to attract new subscribers, but lack of success soon forced him to conclude that he could not extend operation of the library into a second year. Consequently he shut it down as soon as his twelve-month contractual obligation to his charter subscribers was complete.

Rind was fated to be disappointed not only in the operation of this first circulating library, but also with his efforts to abandon it. On April 17, 1764, at 5 PM, at his home in Annapolis, William Rind began auctioning off the books from his library, intending to continue "until they are all disposed of."[8] In this attempt also, however, he failed. Finally, on May 30 he published a broadside announcing a novel plan for selling off his stock of books. He would conduct a lottery in which the prizes would be primarily books and maps, supplemented by some millinery articles which Rind appears to have sold as a sideline. He offered to sell 700 tickets at two dollars apiece, of which 222 would entitle their purchasers to prizes ranging in value from $3 to $100 worth of books and sundries, the values presumably to be determined by Rind himself.

The records do not indicate how Rind fared in this last ingenious effort to recoup some of his equity from his circulating library, but the scheme hardly sounds redolent of success. Two years later Rind moved to Virginia where he died in 1773.[9]

George Wood of Charleston

Whether patterned upon Rind's venture or drawn, as his appears to have been, from contemporary practice in Europe, three other circulating libraries were established in America in the months following the Annapolis experiment. They were all located in cities which were larger in size than Annapolis, and as a result they seemed likely to encounter greater public support. In the order of their establishment, these libraries were located in Charleston, New York, and Boston. Philadelphia's first circulating library was opened in 1767. These four libraries will be reviewed here briefly in that order.

It is not surprising that Charleston in South Carolina was the site of an early circulating library, as that city was one of the leading centers of culture in the Colonial World. Charlestonians were in many respects closer to London than they were to Boston or New York, and they travelled there frequently for business or other reasons. Upon return they consciously strove to emulate the brilliant but brittle foibles of contemporary English society, and manners, habits, and customs in the Carolina town were largely reflective of the Old World. Charleston had had a public library of sorts since, as part of his "Grand Design," the Reverend Thomas Bray and the Society for the Propagation of the Gospel in Foreign Parts established a provincial collection there

PROPOSALS

FOR ESTABLISHING

A CIRCULATING

LIBRARY,

IN *BALTIMORE-TOWN.*

TO point out the advantages of such an institution, by enlarging on the happy influence which good *Books* have on the understanding, by setting forth the countenance which LIBRARIES have received from the *Literati* in all ages, by urging the delight and profit which our youth may reap from having opportunities of reading frequently, under the eye of their parents and friends, the best authors, or, indeed, to expatiate at all, in favour of a well-conducted CIRCULATING LIBRARY, would, to a people much less intelligent than the Inhabitants of this place, be highly unnecessary; the intentional proprietor therefore, after observing that LIBRARIES have become objects of attention in every polite part of *America*, will only inform the Public, that, on being favoured with a suitable number of yearly subscribers, on the conditions undermentioned, he will immediately furnish a *Collection of Books*, not less than eight hundred volumes, by the best authors, with printed catalogues thereof, consisting of

Latin Classics,	*Rhetoric,*	*Adventures,*
History,	*Mathematics,*	*Miscellanies,*
Poetry,	*Astronomy,*	*Novels,*
Religion,	*Geography,*	*Plays,*
Philosophy,	*Chronology,*	*Magazines,*
Physic,	*Cookery,*	*Memoirs,*
Agriculture,	*Voyages,*	*Pamphlets,*
Logic,	*Travels,*	*Essays,*

And every other WORK of *Merit, Erudition* and *true Humour*. The COLLECTION to be occasionally increased with the newest Publications from *London,* &c.

As the advantages of a Library need not be limited to the place where it is established, persons in the country adjacent, becoming subscribers, as is customary, may, with great convenience, be supplied with Books.

CONDITIONS.

1st. Each subscriber to pay four dollars per year, in manner following, viz. one dollar upon their taking out the first book, after the establishment of the Library, of which proper notice will be given; one dollar, six months after; another dollar, nine months after; and the last dollar, at the expiration of the year.

2d. Subscribers in town, to have the privilege of taking books whenever they please, one only at a time.

3d. Subscribers at any distance from Town, to have the additional privilege of taking two books at once.

Other particulars to be communicated when the catalogues are printed.

As the season is advancing when the mind may, with convenience, be gratified and improved with the rational entertainment of reading, those Gentlemen and Ladies disposed to promote this much wished for institution, are requested to be speedy in sending their names, as subscribers, to the *Coffee-House,* the *Fountain-Inn,* and the *Printing-Office,* where subscription papers for the purpose of entering them are kept, that the intentional proprietor may be the sooner enabled to provide an ample collection of books. For the convenience of Gentlemen and Ladies of literary taste and discernment in the country adjacent, subscribers names will also be taken in at Mr. *David Armstrong's,* in the *Forst,* at Mr. *William M'Knight's* Tavern, and at Mr. *Thomas Rickett's,* at *Elk-Ridge,* at which places also, proposals at large may be had gratis.

Joseph Rathell's Broadside Proposing a Circulating Library in Baltimore, 1773 (Orig. 14 x 8⅝ inches). *Courtesy of the Maryland Historical Society* in 1698.[10] Charleston moreover had accorded better treatment to Bray's deposited collection than perhaps any other American city had done, when in the same year the Colonial Assembly appropriated £53 to enable it to function as a true public library serving all citizens.[11] The Charleston Library Society, which is still in existence today, was founded in 1748, and within two years of its founding it could claim fully 130 members. Virtually all fields of knowledge were encompassed within its collections, including science, law, history, and philosophy.[12]

There were also many fine private libraries in Charleston in the middle of the eighteenth century, and many merchants purveyed books along with other merchandise. At least nine, however, stocked large enough inventories of books so that bookselling must have comprised a major part of their livelihood. Robert Wells, Charleston auctioneer and owner of a printing press, claimed in 1771 to have more books for sale than anyone else in America.[13] Isaiah Thomas, who had worked for him as a young journeyman three years earlier, described him as "the principal bookseller for both the Carolinas."[14] Another of these nine—a bookseller of primary importance to this study—was George Wood, Stationer and Book-Binder in Elliott Street.

On February 26, 1763, only sixteen days after Rind had opened his circulating library in Annapolis, George Wood of Charleston announced in the *South Carolina Gazette* that, having imported "a Collection of curious BOOKS, consisting of histories, voyages, travels, lives, memoirs, novels, plays, &c. [he] intended to set on foot A CIRCULATING LIBRARY." As had his fellow-librarian in Maryland, Wood made it clear from the start that he was prepared to serve the reading tastes of both sexes. "Gentlemen and Ladies that approve this plan," he invited, "and are willing to encourage so useful an undertaking, are desired to give in their name."

Little is known of the fate of Wood's circulating library except that it seems to have prospered for some four years. The proprietor pledged that "great care will be taken to add thereto all new books as soon as published," and he appears to have tried to do that. His last specific mention of the library in print was in an advertisement that appeared more than two years later. Using the same description of the collection that he used at its opening, Wood concluded that the books "are lent out to read: the conditions to be observed, and the catalogue, to be seen at his shop."[15] He appears to have kept his lending operation until mid 1767, when on July 20, again using the same phrases that he had used previously to describe his library, he announced that

> He has likewise to dispose of, upwards of one thousand volumes of curious books consisting of histories, voyages, travels, lives, Memoirs, Novels, plays, &c. which he will sell very cheap.
> N.B. Good allowance to schoolmasters.[16]

There is no reason to believe that Wood experienced as much difficulty in selling off his stock as Rind had had in disposing of his. Wood continued his retail bookselling and bookbinding activities in Charleston for many years thereafter.

Garrat Noel of New York

New York was the third Colonial city to have a circulating library. Although New York had not enjoyed the distinguished cultural inheritance of Boston or Charleston, it had nonetheless become an important commercial center by 1763, and a number of good booksellers had established themselves there. William Bradford appears to have sold books from his New York printing office as early as 1693, John Peter Zenger and his wife Catherine both offered their services as stationers in the 1730s and 1740s, and Robert Crommelin opened his bookshop "near the Meal Market" in 1747. The city's two outstanding booksellers, then Whig Hugh Gaine and ever Tory James Rivington, had set up operations in New York in 1751 and 1761 respectively.[17] Also from 1753 forward there was in Dock Street "at the Sign of the Bible" the bookstore of former schoolmaster Garrat Noel who advertised not only books and stationery but also "the very best of Durham Flour of Mustard, and a fresh Parcel of very fine Snuff, commonly called Black Guard,"[18] "the right Tooth Powder, and Stoughton's famous Bitters."[19] It was Noel who, in August 1763, seven months after Rind in Annapolis and six months after Wood in Charleston, opened America's third circulating library.

New York already had a social library at that time, but it was not then available for use. The New-York Society Library had been established by 140 well-to-do citizens in 1754, absorbing the remnants of the old Corporation Library that had been in the custody of James Parker a few years earlier. In 1763, however, the New York City Hall, which housed the Society Library, was temporarily closed for repairs, and it has been suggested that this suspension of "public" library service may have prompted Garrat Noel to open his circulating library.[20]

At any rate, on August 29, 1763, the *New-York Gazette* carried the following announcement:

> To those who delight in Reading, And would spend their Leisure Hours, and Winter Evenings, with Profit and Entertainment, THIS IS TO GIVE NOTICE, that this Day is opened by GARRAT NOEL, Bookseller next Door to the Merchants Coffee-House, A CIRCULATING LIBRARY: Consisting of several Thousand Volumes of Choice Books, in History, Divinity, Travels, Voyages, Novels, &c.

The terms for Noel's circulating library were quite similar to those for Rind's. The subscription fee was Five Dollars (later Four) per year; one book could be borrowed at a time; all damages were to be paid by the borrower. Books could be obtained "out of the Library any Time, except Sunday, and after Store is shut."[21]

That single statement may account for much of the popularity of circulating libraries during the ensuing century. Whereas most social and other "public" libraries of the time stood apart from other agencies and therefore could afford to be staffed only two or three hours weekly, circulating libraries were almost always operated as adjuncts to other activities, such as bookselling, which were attended by their proprietors throughout the day. Thus heavy readers, or those who were not able to discipline their personal regimens to meet the limited service hours of social libraries, found the extended schedules of the circulating libraries to be highly convenient.

Noel published a catalogue of his library, which he handed out gratis to his subscribers. Regrettably, however, no copies of the catalogue have been preserved, so his holdings can no longer be evaluated. It is known that he added to his collection regularly, the first such accession announced only two weeks after he opened. He also pledged to obtain "all new published Books, Pamphlets, Magazines, and Reviews, &c."[22]

Despite Noel's efforts, however, his circulating library appears to have languished; at least it was not able to sustain itself in the face of the competition of the Society Library when the renovated City Hall reopened a year later. Both the reopened Society Library and Noel's library were noticed in the *New-York Gazette* of September 19, 1765. Noel's was advertised again a week later, but thereafter there is no more mention of his circulating library. In a public announcement three years later Noel offered to re-establish his project "upon a very extensive Plan,"[23] but this last effort appears also to have come to naught. He continued to sell books in New York until 1776,[24] the year of his death, but his short tenure as proprietor of a circulating library—like Rind, only long enough to fulfill his obligations to his charter subscribers—may be taken as sure indication that his book-lending venture was not financially successful.

John Mein of Boston

Boston, which claimed to be the second leading book-trade center of the English-speaking world, saw its first commercial library opened in 1765. Its proprietor, John Mein, had arrived in Boston from Edinburgh a year earlier and had opened a bookstall "nearly opposite to Bromfield's Lane, Marlboro'-Street." At first he sold not only books but also "excellent bottl'd Bristol beer near two years old."[25] Twelve months later Mein removed his bookselling activities to better quarters "at the LONDON BOOK-STORE (lately improved by Messi'rs. *Rivington* and *Miller*) the second Door above the BRITISH Coffee-House, North Side of King-street."[26] Also, noting that such establishments had "been hitherto unattempted in New-England," Mein opened his circulating library at this stand on October 31, 1765.

Mein claimed to have some twelve hundred volumes in his library at the time of its opening. The conditions to be observed by its subscribers were again quite similar to those exacted by Rind and Noel. The annual subscription fee was £1-8, although six-month subscriptions could be purchased for Eighteen Shillings, and quarterly access could be got for 10s 8d. The library was open daily, with the probable exception of Sundays, from 10 until 1 and from 3 until 6 o'clock.[27]

Mein's announcement to the readers of the *Massachusetts Gazette* summarizes faithfully the functions of such establishments as viewed by the contemporary reading public.

Something of this kind has been long wanted to amuse the *Man of Leisure*; to afford an elegant and agreeable relaxation to the minds of *Men of business*, and to insinuate knowledge and instruction, under the veil of entertainment to the FAIR SEX—here likewise the *Divine* and the *Christian* may find in the works of the *Pious* and the *Learned*, that exalted satisfaction, which flows from the serious study of the *Christian Religion*—the *Marchant* may meet with a complete history and description of those countries to which he has traded; which may open to him new prospects of advantage, while he indulges a laudable curiosity—the *Student of Physic* will have an opportunity of perusing some of the best books in physic and surgery; and the *Physician*, of corroborating his own experience, from the judicious observations and practice of the most noted medical Authors—the *Man* who delights in speculation and solitude, may retire with his favourite authors, into the calm and venerable regions of *Philosophy*: And, *Those* to whom a lighter sort of literary amusement is necessary, will here always find an opportunity of employing their leisure hours with entertainment and satisfaction— the *man of Taste* and *Sentiment*, in the company of his Shakespear and other dramatic and poetical authors, seized with the noble and genuine enthusiasm of *Poetry*, may enjoy all the pleasure—the painful pleasures attending an exquisite sensibility.[28]

Mein attempted to lay in a stock of books that would enable his library to fulfill these diverse functions— technical, inspirational, cultural, educational, and recreational—this last term only beginning then to come into the English language. A copy of his 57-page catalogue, which Mein issued upon opening his library and sold for a Shilling, has been preserved in the Massachusetts Historical Society. Of the some 700 titles listed therein, more than a third would be classed as religion and philosophy, but there are also present some eighty titles in science and technology, mostly medicine, and a number of standard works in commerce, political economy, and law. About a fourth of the collection comprises literature and fiction, including the 1762 London edition of *Joe Miller's Jests*, and there are healthy representations of travel, history, and biography. Some thirty-seven titles, most of which are novels, are in French.

No evidence can be adduced as to the financial success or failure of John Mein's circulating library. He continued printing and bookselling in Boston for some six years thereafter, but whether with or without a library cannot be determined. Mein's sojourn in Boston was a stormy one. On one occasion his store was mobbed because of his loyalist sympathies, and in the scuffle Mein shot a grenadier. Financial reverses hounded him constantly, and he languished for a time in debtor's prison. In 1771 Mein removed permanently to England.[29]

Lewis Nicola of Philadelphia

If Boston was British America's foremost booktrade center in the 1760s, Philadelphia was most certainly its second. Commerce in books had increased markedly there since 1723, when Franklin could claim, not wholly accurately, that there was "not a good Bookseller's Shop in any of the Colonies Southward of Boston."[30] Some forty-two printers worked in Philadelphia between 1740 and the Revolution, and the products of their presses were extensive and varied. Philadelphia was perhaps better equipped with libraries than any other Colonial city. The Library Company, established in 1731, was by this time securely fixed and widely patronized. Other social libraries—the Amicable, the Association, and the Union—were to be absorbed by it in 1768.[31] The Loganian Library had been opened for public use in 1760 but its highly erudite collections attracted only occasional readers. There were also special libraries: the Carpenter's Company had been assembling a collection of technical books in its field of interest for some three decades, and the Assembly had maintained a library of laws and statutes for two.

There was nonetheless in Philadelphia an unmet need for certain kinds of literature. Social historian Carl Bridenbaugh describes it as follows:

> Increasing leisure among certain classes in the city, as well as among the ladies, and a desire to fill it with light and entertaining reading, paved the way for the establishment of circulating libraries, whence booksellers dispensed to subscribers "a considerable List of Novel Writers, whose depictive Talents" as expounded by the canny Robert Bell, "tends to dignify the human Mind, by an Abundance of recreative and instructive Entertainment, calculated to guide the Youth of both sexes through the dangerous Whirlpool of agitated Passions."[32]

This need attracted the attention of Lewis Nicola, a bookseller who had maintained a stand on Second Street between Race and Vine since 1765.[33] On September 10, 1767, Nicola announced in the *Pennsylvania Journal* his intention to open a "New Circulating Library" at that location. It is not clear whether the word "New" was simply part of the name of the establishment or was intended to distinguish it from a similar operation that had preceded it in time. If it meant the latter, which certainly seems to be the more reasonable of the two interpretations, this is the only extant indication that there was an earlier library in the city. At any rate, four days after his announcement Nicola's New Circulating Library was in business.[34]

Nicola's library contained between three and four hundred volumes at time of opening, heavily weighted toward history, fiction, poetry, plays, and travel literature. Among books specifically mentioned by the proprietor as being in stock were "Female American, Emera or Fair American, Pittsborough, Neck or Nothing;" a few well-chosen French books; the travels of Byron, Sharp, and Smollett; and the *Memoirs* of the Duke of Cumberland. These first titles could hardly be considered a distinguished lot for the time, and it is difficult to understand just why Nicola singled them out for special mention.[35] The library was a success, however. Within two years it could advertise more than 500 volumes, by 1770 it had "upwards of 700 volumes," and by 1771 it had grown to more than 1,000.[36]

When he first opened his New Circulating Library, Nicola imposed one requirement that had not previously been seen in the American Colonies: he required a deposit of £3 from each subscriber in addition to an annual fee of $3. The deposit, which apparently was returned upon termination of the subscription, may have been to guarantee the return of books borrowed. Since his later advertisements make no mention of a deposit, he may have given up the idea. He soon lowered the subscription fee also to Two Dollars per year, Ten Shillings for six months, or Six Shillings per quarter, which must have been quite a bargain for access to a collection of books the size he claimed to have. In view of the fact that his library thrived and grew for several years, this low subscription rate may have indicated that the library enjoyed a considerable patronage. Nicola also instituted another practice which later became standard among American circulating libraries: he would rent books to nonsubscribers for Sixpence weekly plus a deposit equal to the value of the book.

It appears that Nicola produced a printed catalogue of his library, but no copies of it are known to exist today. His library was open daily save Sundays; borrowers could withdraw one book at a time and exchange it daily or keep it for up to four weeks. The proprietor found it necessary to move his library several times. In 1768 he was in Market Street. Late in 1769 he removed "to the Corner of Lawrence's Court, in Spruce-Street between Second and Third," where he also changed the name of his establishment to the General Circulating Library. A year later he relocated on Third Street, three doors below Spruce, and a year after that he moved again, this time to "the Green Lamp, on the south side of Chestnut-Street, the second door from the corner of Second-street."[37] The timing of these changes in location suggest that Nicola held annual leases to his several stands.

An important inference may be drawn from Nicola's last two addresses mentioned above. In both locations, his General Circulating Library shared premises with Ellenor Fitzgerald, a milliner who advertised "HATS, BONNET, CLOAKS, &c. at the shortest notice, and in the newest fashion. Silk stockings washed and stoved . . . sarsenets, blonds and clear starching."[38] This merging of the two businesses in the same quarters bespeaks a heavily female clientele for the library, which should not surprise when it is recalled that women were at that time debarred "from the masculine confines of the Library Company or the Loganian Collection, and from consultation of law-books at the State House or scientific treatises at the Hospital."[39] For the same reason such cohabitation by millinery shops and circulating libraries was not an uncommon phenomenon in other cities in the decades that followed.

The ultimate disposition of the General Circulating Library is not known. Nicola's last recorded address in Philadelphia was in 1791; he was then "at the Debtor's Apartment."[40]

And Others . . .

Besides Rind, Wood, Noel, Mein, and Nicola, at least six other individuals attempted to establish circulating libraries in the British Colonies in America before the Revolution. At best, however, these efforts saw only indifferent success. It is interesting to note that five of the six were located in the cities that had already enjoyed the circulating libraries discussed above. Baltimore was the only additional city where such an establishment was proposed during the pre-War years, and that effort aborted.

In point of time the next circulating library to be established following Nicola's opening was in direct competition with him. On September 21, 1769, Philadelphia printer Thomas Bradford announced a library at his house on Second Street near Arch.[41] He published a catalogue of his holdings which he distributed gratis, but no copies of it have been preserved. Although the fate of Bradford's Circulating Library is not known, it appears to have flourished at least until 1773. The proprietor, however, continued his printing office well into the next century.

In Charleston meanwhile one Samuel Gifford, *"Lately arrived from* London, *Acquaint[ed] Ladies and Gentlemen . . ."* in November of 1772 that he had opened a circulating library at a store in Broad Street, three doors from Gadsden's Alley which he would attend daily from 10 AM until noon and from 2 until 5 PM. His terms were quite similar to those already seen elsewhere. His annual fee was One Pound Sterling, allowing one book to be borrowed at a time, which could be exchanged daily or kept up to a month. An exception to the circulation period was that "No subscriber [was] to keep any New Book longer than four days," suggesting that the demand for the latest publications could be as brisk then as it can now.[42] Gifford never advertised his library again after his first announcement, and it appears to have gone soon out of business.

Annapolis got its second circulating library in early July 1773, when immigrant Scot William Aikman opened his 1,200-volume collection to any subscriber who would pay One Guinea per year, the same fee charged by Rind for access to his much smaller library a decade earlier. Aikman would also hire out his books to nonsubscribers at Three Pence overnight. He attended the library daily from 8 AM until 8 PM and circulated one book at a time for periods ranging from one to fourteen days.[43] He also sold "Old Port Wine of the best quality, London porter, ale and Cheshire cheese."[44] Aikman issued a catalogue of his library, of which an imperfect volume in the Maryland Historical Society is presumed to be a copy. Almost half of the titles listed in it are literature or fiction, and another third comprises history, biography, and books of travel. There is only a slight representation of theology, plus a smattering of political economy, law, technology, rhetoric, philosophy, and miscellany. It was a good collection of the popular books of the period. In November 1773 Aikman indicated his intention to place his library "upon a footing, if not superior to any circulating library on the continent."[45] He also contracted with a Baltimore merchant to provide a delivery outlet for his books in that city,[46] but thereafter no further mention of the library ever appeared, so again it is not possible to determine its ultimate disposition. Because of his loyalist leanings, Aikman by 1775 found Maryland somewhat inhospitable, and he departed for Jamaica where he worked as a printer-bookseller until his death nine years later.

Aikman's attempt to establish a Baltimore connection in 1773 appears to have been prompted by an effort at the time by one Joseph Rathell to develop a full circulating library in that city. Rathell, a lecturer and schoolmaster, announced to the public on October 16, 1773,[47] that he contemplated such a venture, and a week later he distributed a broadside proposal[48] inviting subscriptions. Within a month, however, it had become clear that there was inadequate support from the public for the plan to succeed, perhaps because of Aikman's already existing delivery of books to Baltimore readers, and Rathell abandoned it completely. Baltimore would have to wait until after the War for its first circulating library.

Bookseller Samuel Loudon was the person responsible for New York's second circulating library. He opened his operation on the first day of the year 1774,[49] and some three weeks later distributed gratis to subscribers a catalogue of his holdings.[50] It is to be regretted that no copies of the catalogue appear any longer to be extant. In November he issued a new catalogue of "upwards of a thousand volumes,"[51] but no copies of that second catalogue exist today either. In the advertisement for the second catalogue, Loudon observed that "the ladies are his best customers, and shew a becoming delicacy of taste in their choice of books." He quickly added, however, that "neither are the gentlemen deficient in shewing the ladies a laudable example in this respect." The library, which was "open every week day, from morning till night" cost subscribers Twenty Shillings per year, and others "one penny for each shilling

Bookplate from William Aikman's Circulating Library in Annapolis, 1773-1775 (Orig. 4½ x 3½ inches). *Courtesy of the American Antiquarian Society*

the book they read is valued at." Loudon indicated his willingness to purchase or trade "for any old library or parcel of books, particularly for history and well chosen novels, for the use of the Library." His operation prospered and by early 1776 he could claim to have more than two thousand volumes,[52] easily the largest circulating library in America. "Decidedly a whig," to use Isaiah Thomas' description of him, Loudon departed New York when the British troops entered the city in September,[53] and thereafter there is no further mention of his circulating library until 1785.[54]

The last circulating library to be established in Colonial America was the property of the enterprising and resourceful bookseller, publisher, book auctioneer, printer, and binder, Robert Bell, who came from Scotland via Dublin in 1767 and began business in Philadelphia. In 1774 Bell announced that he was entering the field with his Universal Circulating Library to be located in the old Union Library quarters in Third Street.[55] Bell published a catalogue of the books in his library in 1778 listing some 2,000 volumes,[56] but no copies appear to exist today, and little is known about the fate of this collection.

Summary

Thus eleven circulating libraries had been proposed or established in six Colonial cities during the fourteen years immediately preceding the Revolution (See Table 1). Some never got beyond the proposal stage, and others were opened but then failed. Some, however, appear to have sustained a fair amount of patronage and doubtless brought to their proprietors some of the profit for which they were intended. There is evidence that Wood's and Aikman's libraries were probably successful, as were Nicola's and Loudon's to be sure.

TABLE 1.

Colonial Period Circulating Libraries

Proprietor	Location	Founded	Annual Fee	No. of Vols.	Longevity (Mos.)
William Rind	Annapolis	1763	£1-1	150+	12
George Wood	Charleston	1763		1,000	48
Garrat Noel	New York	1763	$5	3,000?	12?
John Mein	Boston	1765	£1-8	1,200	
Lewis Nicola	Philadelphia	1767	$3-$2	400-1,000	51+
Thomas Bradford	Philadelphia	1769	£1		45+
Samuel Gifford	Charleston	1772	£1		
William Aikman	Annapolis	1773	£1-1	1,200	4-26
Joseph Rathell	Baltimore	1773	$4	800+	0
Samuel Loudon	New York	1774	£1	1,000-2,000	32+
Robert Bell	Philadelphia	1774		2,000	48+

By the end of the period a rather standard library practice had come into being. Subscription rates varied a little from one location to another, but in other respects conditions governing their operation and use had much in common. Printed catalogues were generally in use, circulation periods did not vary much, hours of opening were largely similar. The more successful libraries stocked upwards of a thousand volumes.

The collections of the circulating libraries, although diverse in their contents, were nonetheless very heavily weighted toward fiction and literature, and only slightly less so to biography, history, and books of travel. Their proprietors strove to make it clear that they catered not only to men but also to women, a claim which few other contemporary libraries could make. They appear by the time the War began to have made a more or less permanent place for themselves on the American cultural scene.

REFERENCES

1. Lawrence C. Wroth, *History of Printing in Colonial Maryland* (Baltimore: Typothetae, 1922), p. 85.
2. Joseph T. Wheeler, "Booksellers and Circulating Libraries in Colonial Maryland," *Maryland Historical Magazine* 34 (June 1939): 113.
3. Henry Callister to William Rind, September 20, 1762, in Henry Callister letterbook 3: 579.
4. Mary V. Moore, "Circulating Libraries in the Southeastern United States, 1762-1842" (masters thesis, University of North Carolina, 1958), pp. 29-30.
5. *Maryland Gazette*, January 13, 1763.
6. Ibid., February 10, 1763.
7. Ibid., January 13, 1763.
8. Ibid., April 5, 1764.
9. Wroth, *History of Printing*, p. 85.
10. Charles T. Laugher, *Thomas Bray's Grand Design* (Chicago: American Library Association, 1973), p. 38.

11. Elizabeth W. Stone, *American Library Development, 1600-1899* (N.Y.: H. W. Wilson Co., 1977), p. 127.

12. Frederick P. Bowes, *The Culture of Early Charleston* (Chapel Hill: University of North Carolina Press, 1942), p. 54.

13. Hennig Cohen, *The South Carolina Gazette, 1732-1775* (Columbia: University of South Carolina Press, 1953), p. 123.

14. Isaiah Thomas, *History of Printing in America* (New York: Weathervane, 1970), p. 570.

15. *South Carolina Gazette*, April 27, 1765.

16. Ibid., July 20, 1767.

17. Edwin D. Hoffman, "The Bookshops of New York City, 1743-1948," *New York History* 30 (January 1949): 53.

18. *New-York Gazette*, August 29, 1763.

19. Austin B. Keep, *History of the New York Society Library* (New York: DeVinne Press, 1908), p. 102.

20. Ibid., p. 103.

21. *New-York Gazette*, September 12, 1763.

22. Ibid.

23. *New-York Journal*, September 1, 1768.

24. Keep, *History* . . . , p. 107.

25. John E. Alden, "John Mein, Publisher: an Essay in Bibliographic Detection," *Bibliographical Society of America Papers* 36 (1942): 199.

26. *Boston Gazette*, October 7, 1765.

27. *Massachusetts Gazette*, October 31, 1765.

28. Ibid.

29. Charles K. Bolton, "Circulating Libraries in Boston, 1765-1865," *Publications of the Colonial Society of Massachusetts* 11 (February 1907): 200.

30. *Autobiography*, ed. L. W. Labaree (New Haven: Yale University Press, 1964), p. 141.

31. E. V. Lamberton, "Colonial Libraries of Pennsylvania," *Pennsylvania Magazine of History and Biography* 42 (1918): 193-234.

32. "Press and Book in Eighteenth-Century Philadelphia," *Pennsylvania Magazine of History and Biography* 65 (January 1941): 20-21.

33. H. Glenn Brown and Maude O. Brown, *Directory of the Book-Arts and Book Trade in Philadelphia to 1820* (New York: New York Public Library, 1950), p. 89.

34. *Pennsylvania Chronicle*, September 14, 1767; ". . . opening this day, A NEW CIRCULATING LIBRARY."

35. The anonymous *Adventures of Emmera, or the Fair American*, a novel attributed to Arthur Young, had been published in London in 1767. *Female American*, a pseudonymous work by one "Unca Eliza Winkfield," had appeared there in the same year. *Neck or Nothing*, a two-act farce by David Garrick, had been published a year earlier.

36. *Pennsylvania Gazette*, January 12, 1769; *Pennsylvania Chronicle*, January 8, 1770; *Pennsylvania Gazette*, January 3, 1771.

37. Thomas, *History of Printing*, p. 429; *Pennsylvania Chronicle*, December 4, 1769; *Pennsylvania Gazette*, January 3, 1771; *Pennsylvania Packet*, December 23, 1771.

38. Ellenor Fitzgerald's removal notice appears alongside that of the General Circulating Library in the *Pennsylvania Packet*, December 23, 1771.

39. Bridenbaugh, "Press and Book," p. 27.

40. Brown, *Directory*, p. 89.

41. *Pennsylvania Journal*.

42. *South Carolina Gazette*, November 12, 1772.

43. *Maryland Gazette*, July 1, 1773.

44. Wheeler, "Booksellers and Circulating Libraries," p. 126.

45. *Maryland Gazette*, November 11, 1773.

46. *Maryland Journal and Baltimore Advertiser*, October 23-30, 1773.

47. Ibid.

48. A copy of this broadside is preserved in the Maryland Historical Society.

49. *Rivington's New-York Gazetteer*, December 30, 1773.

50. *New-York Gazette and Weekly Mercury*, January 24, 1774.

51. Ibid., November 21, 1774.

52. *New-York Packet, and the American Advertiser*, January 4, 1776.

53. *History of Printing*, p. 482.

54. George L. McKay, "A Register of Artists, Booksellers, Printers and Publishers in New York City, 1781-1800," *Bulletin of the New York Public Library* 45 (1941): 489.

55. *Pennsylvania Packet*, March 14, 1774.

56. This catalogue is advertised in Bell's 1778 printing of Johann Georg von Zimmerman's *Strictures on National Pride*.

Chapter Three
Consolidation and Growth, to the End of the Century

I f the period before the Revolution was one of innovation and testing for circulating libraries, the seven-
teen years between the cessation of the War and the end
of the century was one of consolidation of practice and
growth in both their size and number. By 1800 circulating libraries had come to be an expected part of the cultural apparatus of every self-respecting community. The
national thrust to read was strong, and the profit motive
was there to help accommodate it.

American Reading Interests

The American appetite for reading abated not a whit
in the years following the Revolution. The number of
books currently being printed in the new nation was
soon substantially higher than the number that had
been printed in the Colonies. Hostilities had barely
ceased before book importation recommenced, but at a
vastly accelerated pace. The number of newspapers being produced in America's towns increased rapidly.
New social libraries were established in growing numbers; where Shera was able to identify 51 in New England before 1780, he located 325 more before the end of
the century.[1]

Although America's catholicity of reading taste also
continued into this period, there were some noted shifts
in preference, as indicated in Table 2.[2] These figures,
to be fully understood, must be compared to the con-
current population increase of 190 percent and the
overall rise in American book production of 400 percent.

TABLE 2

Subjects of American Printed Works, 1778-1798

	Litera- ture	Medi- cine	Music	Theol- ogy	Social Science	Political Science
1778	17	7	8	37	15	12
1798	203	38	16	244	62	143
Percent of increase	1200	550	200	660	400	1200

Clearly the kinds of books which enjoyed the most disproportionate gains in popularity during the two decades were *belles-lettres* and political science.

Interest in political matters, nourished prior to the War by the events leading to the separation of the Colonies from Great Britain, had received its greatest impetus with the appearance in 1776 of Thomas Paine's *Common Sense.* An estimated 150,000 copies of this phenomenal treatise were sold during its first year alone, and it continued to be read widely for a long time thereafter. Equally important perhaps is the fact that it inspired even wider interest in political affairs than had existed before and led to the extensive popularity of such later works as Paine's *Rights of Man, The Federalist,* and Jefferson's *Notes on the State of Virginia,* as well as the reading of a host of little-known and obscure political tracts and pamphlets. It also contributed to a wide interest in books of a quasi-political character: recent history, memoirs and biographies of political figures, and even such political novels as Fénelon's *Télémaque,* which was long a stock item in every bookstore and library in the land.

The even more prodigious increase in novel reading during the period cannot, in fact, be wholly separated from the political temper of the time. The American Revolution, as all revolutions, had much of romanticism in it, and this romanticism displayed itself unselfconsciously in the flood of fiction that swept American readers before it. Most of this fiction came out of England, but not all of it, as is attested by the American popularity of Goethe's *Sorrows of Young Werther* (1774) and Rousseau's *Emile* (1762).

It was *Emile*, in fact, that blazed the way for other educational fiction of the time, including Thomas Day's *Sandford and Merton* (1789) and Elizabeth Inchbald's *Simple Story* (1791) and *Nature and Art* (1796), all of which attempted to demonstrate the ability of educational change to accomplish social reform.

Radical political thinkers meanwhile vocalized their thoughts on reform through novels which they too contributed to this rising tide of fiction. Thomas Holcroft's *Anna St. Ives* (1792) and *Hugh Trevor* (1794) were standard fare among American readers, as were also William Godwin's *Caleb Williams* (1794) and *St. Leon* (1799), all veiled advocates of social change. His wife Mary Wollstonecraft wrote two novels of this kind, *Mary, a Fiction* (1788) and *The Wrongs of Women* (1798), the latter six years after her *Vindication of the Rights of Women*. Robert Bage's *Hermsprong* (1796) belongs in this category, as does Charlotte Smith's *Desmond* (1792), wherein she sends the hero to France, giving her opportunity through the mouths of her characters to discuss key issues of revolution and government.

Romantic revolt against constraints of both nature and contemporary realism gave rise also during this time to the Gothic novel, usually said to have begun in 1765 with Horace Walpole's *Castle of Otranto*. The number of popular tales that built thereafter upon terror, horror, and preternatural effects was very large, embracing Charlotte Smith's *Old Manor House* (1793), Mrs. Ann Radcliffe's *Mysteries of Udolpho* (1794), and Matthew

Gregory Lewis' *The Monk* (1796). Revolt against geographical constraints prompted such Oriental settings for fiction as was utilized by William Beckford in *Vathek* (1787).

American creative writers were also coming to be heard from during this period. Susanna Rawson's *Charlotte Temple* (1791) was extremely popular. Hannah Foster's *Coquette* (1797), Hugh Brackenridge's picaresque *Modern Chivalry* (1792 and after), Charles Brockden Brown's Gothic tale *Wieland* (1798), and his philosophical novel *Ormond* (1799) all found their places in the hearts and minds of America's reading public. Plays also were not only seen but read widely, including those by American dramatists Royall Tyler, William Dunlap, and others.

But these are the great names, and to cite them alone is to present a distorted picture of the novels that consumed, and were consumed by, eighteenth-century American citizens. By far the larger number of fictional works read during the period are practically unheard of today. Some, in fact, are totally unheard of, defying completely latter-day efforts to identify them bibliographically. Popular though the aforementioned titles were, they were grossly outnumbered on the shelves of bookshops and libraries by often anonymous novels with such titles as *The Algerine Spy, Batteridge, Calista, Count Roderic's Castle, Excessive Sensibility, Fanny Meadows, Female Frailty, Generosity, Girl of the Mountains, Hapless Orphan, Irish Excursion, Mortimore Castle, Offspring of Fancy, Orphan Swains, Parson's Wife, Peggy and Patty, Posthumous Daughter, Raynsford Park, Shrine of Bertha, Subterranean Cavern, Sutton Abbey, Villeroy, Woodland Cottage, Zoriada,* and a thousand others. One hardly needs to read them today, but they were widely read in their time.

Booksellers and other merchants were diligent in their efforts to profit from this burgeoning national motivation to read, and one key method of doing so was by extending circulating library service to potential readers whose needs had for one reason or another gone previously unmet. One anonymous but knowledgeable observer, writing in 1789, had the following to say about libraries in North America:

> It is scarce possible to conceive the number of readers with which even every little town abounds. The common people are on a footing, in point of literature, with the middle ranks in Europe. They all read and write, and understand arithmetic;—almost every little town now furnishes a circulating library.[3]

Circulating library proprietors modified their book collections during this period to meet changes in the public taste, and some libraries even developed specialized holdings for special clienteles. Libraries sometimes came during this period to be attached to other kinds of mercantile stands so as to facilitate their accessibility and use by patrons. A few limited innovations also came into circulating library practice during these years, although for the most part the time was one of consolidation and extension rather than one of experimentation and change.

At least thirty-nine new circulating libraries were opened or proposed in nineteen different cities between the end of the War and 1800. Spreading north, south, and west, circulating libraries came to New Hampshire in 1796, to Georgia in 1798, and to the Trans-Allegheny west also in 1798. To the north Samuel Larkin, bookseller of Portsmouth, offered up some seven hundred titles "for sale or circulation" in 1796. Subscriptions cost Two Dollars per quarter, or nonsubscribers could rent duodecimos for 8 Cents or octavos for 12½ Cents weekly.[4] George Lamb's prices were higher in the south when he opened a library in conjunction with his general store in Savannah two years later. Duodecimos there brought 10 Cents weekly and octavos 18¾ Cents, and quarterly subscriptions cost Three Dollars. Lamb died the following year, however, and the later destiny of his library is not known.[5] In the west John Boyd contemplated founding a circulating library in Pittsburgh in 1788,[6] but he committed suicide two weeks later, "a fate," opines Wright, "which has tempted more than one library promoter."[7] By 1798, however, John Gilkison was operating a circulating library there in his bookstore.[8] Other towns to gain circulating libraries for the first time in the eighteenth century include Baltimore (at last in 1784), Providence (1789), Alexandria (1792), Georgetown (1792), New London (1793), Newburyport and Salem (1794), Norwich (1796), Newport (1798), as well as Fairhaven, Massachusetts and Lancaster (1800). All of the towns moreover that had had circulating libraries before the War had them also, often in multiple numbers, in the Post-War period.

Not only did circulating librarians extend their services to new locations during this period but they also enlarged and modified their holdings in accord with their patrons' wishes. Whereas the median size of the circulating libraries for which catalogues are still extant from the period 1765-1789 was 718 titles, the number in the following decade almost doubled to 1,413. It should be noted here that these are *titles* and not *volumes*. The ratio of volumes to titles in the circulating library collections of this time frequently ran as high as two to one and sometimes even higher. Thus the typical libraries of the period might be said to have ranged from 1,500 to 3,000 volumes, but with one collection to be discussed in detail later, claiming to have ten times that number! The subject composition of the collections for which catalogues exist also changed notably in one important regard during this period. The median percentage of the collections which constituted fiction was twenty-seven in the years 1765-1789, but it increased dramatically to thirty-seven in the subsequent decade, bespeaking clearly the rising popularity of the novel among American readers. This rise in the representation of fiction in circulating libraries continued steeply upward through the first quarter of the nineteenth century also. Other shifts in the subject composition of the collections at this time, however, were either slight or caused by local conditions which cannot now be easily interpreted. Details are given in Appendix II at the back of this volume.

Another evidence of the efforts by merchants to bring rental books to readers in these years was the establishment of circulating libraries in emporiums other than bookstores. As was mentioned above, George Lamb operated a circulating library in his general store in Savannah. Foster, Drown & Co. of Providence were druggists in addition to maintaining a library in 1789. William Martin sold dry goods and confectionary at 45 Main Street in Boston, where he also ran a circulating library. John Chalk kept a two-thousand-volume library in his "Musical Repository" in Philadelphia, where he also advertised "fine flavoured Imperial, young Hyson, Hyson, Hyson Skin, and Souchong Tea."[9] In 1792 John Lockwood's thousand-volume collection in Georgetown was located in Suter's Tavern. At the end of the century John M'Donald of Philadelphia was tending a library in his brokerage firm. Locations of circulating libraries appear to have been determined by the ease of their accessibility to the public, the availability of someone to man the library throughout the day, and the relative cost of the space.

Except for their understandable concentration on fast-moving fiction and *belles-lettres*, commercial lending libraries seem very seldom to have focused their collecting activities on particular subjects as did a fair number of the social libraries of the time. A single exception shows up in the few that catered heavily or exclusively to foreign-speaking clienteles. The longstanding German community in Philadelphia and environs appears to have been large enough to warrant such treatment. Jacob Lahn kept a German Circulating Library there, with over a thousand volumes of "the best German authors," on Fourth Street between Race and Vine for a year or two following 1785.[10] Doubtless the largest foreign-language circulating library in the young nation was the one established in Lancaster in 1800 by Christian Jacob Hütter; within six months of its opening he claimed to have some four thousand volumes.[11] The large recent contingent of émigrés that settled in Philadelphia following the French Revolution[12] was served beginning in 1797 by Joseph de la Grange's French Circulating Library of 1,500 volumes at 110 Walnut Street.[13] Except in such cases, the representation of foreign-language books in circulating libraries was slight, sometimes embracing a few Latin classics, a handful of standard French works and a few titles in German. In special situations there might be more. For example, Jacob D. Dietrick of Hagerstown, a city with a large German-speaking population, stocked about ten percent German books in the circulating library which he maintained "adjoining his Book, Paint, & Hardware Store." Approximately one-sixth of the collection in Hocquet Caritat's huge library in New York, about which more will be said later, was in the French language, but with

(51)

a very few such outstanding exceptions, the stock-in-trade of the circulating libraries was understandably in *English*.

Some Major Circulating Libraries

Although a number of the *fin-de-siècle* commercial lending libraries were weak, some unable even to survive the proposal stage, several others were very extensive and became major cultural forces in the communities which they served. Those singled out for fuller treatment here, not because they were representative but rather because they were highly influential, are the establishments of John Dabney of Salem, William P. Blake of Boston, and Hocquet Caritat of New York.

John Dabney.[14] Born in Boston in 1752, John Dabney had been one of the founders of the *Salem Mercury* in 1786, but he left the newspaper three years later to open a bookstore and Salem's first circulating library. Salem had a very strong Social Library at the time, but aside from a few plays and fewer novels, its holdings tended more to instruct than to entertain or amuse, and it was this deficiency that Dabney set out to repair. He began with a relatively modest library of some 750 titles well selected with an eye to popularity, and he enjoyed brisk patronage from the start. Fiction and *belles-lettres*, including almost a hundred plays, comprised two-thirds of the listings in his first *Catalogue of Books, for Sale or Circulation, in Town or Country*, which he had printed in 1791. He seems at first not to have taken subscriptions to his "Salem Circulating Library," preferring rather to rent out books at 9 Cents weekly for quartos, 7 Cents for octavos, 4 Cents for duodecimos, and 2 Cents for periodicals, pamphlets, and plays. By 1801 he had increased his rental prices by half, and he was also by then accepting subscribers at Two Dollars for three months.

In addition to his rental business and the retail selling of new and secondhand books, Dabney also operated a bookbindery and a lottery office, and he served as postmaster from 1790 to 1815. He also trafficked in materia medica. He maintained a standing offer of "Cash Paid for Books," and he also advertised "Books Exchanged for Books," both calculated to bring continuing variety to his shelves. He stocked mariners' maps and charts, children's books, and "Classics of every kind—English, French, Latin, and Greek for the use of Academies, Schools, and Individuals, in large and small quantities."[15]

Dabney's library flourished for thirty years, outlasting at least three other circulating libraries that were established in Salem in the meantime. In 1794 Dabney issued a supplemental listing of recent accessions which was even larger than his complete catalogue had been three years earlier. In 1801 he produced his last known catalogue of some 1,770 titles, one of the largest circulating libraries in the nation to that time. When he retired in 1818 his library contained about eight thousand volumes, still heavily fiction.

Dabney died in 1819, but his impact on the town of Salem lasted long thereafter. A contemporary wrote at the time of his death:

> When he first opened a Book-store in Salem, anything deserving the name was unknown. A few books in common use might be bought & other books must be bought in Boston, or if of any character, imported. Dabney began as if we were readers of a higher class, as if we read from our enquiries & not in books long used and by the wise forgotten.[16]

In noting his passing, the *Salem Register* spoke of his early years in the circulating library:

John Dabney, Circulating Library Proprietor of Salem, Massachusetts, 1752-1819. *Courtesy of the Essex Institute, Salem, Mass.*

He had a collection of the best authors as was then to be found in this part of the country. . . . The advantages to the town have been felt in all the departments of literature, in all the conveniences of the press, and in all our establishments for the promotion of knowledge and letters.[17]

William P. Blake.[18] Meanwhile in 1792 William P. Blake took over Benjamin Guild's circulating library and Boston Book Store. Guild, a well-connected Harvard graduate, had operated the establishment for some seven years and had developed a collection of considerable literary distinction by the time of his death. Guild issued catalogues of books "to be Let or Sold" in 1788, 1789, and 1791, but since all three were avowedly selective rather than complete, it is dangerous to attempt to analyze their subject content. It appears, however, that fiction may never have constituted more than a third of his holdings.

If that inference is accurate, then Blake must have set about immediately upon taking over the library to increase the representation of novels on his shelves. He published catalogues in 1793, 1796, 1798, and 1800, and they show a steady increase in fiction, comprising 37, 50, 54, and 63 percent respectively of the titles listed. They also indicate a marked decline in his holdings of religion and philosophy over the same period.

In 1796 Blake removed his library to better quarters at No.1 Cornhill, at the northeastern corner of Spring Lane, and two years later his brother Lemuel joined him in the venture. The library reportedly "acquired a reputation," "enjoyed a period of prosperity," and "soon inspired imitators."[19] The size of the collection increased steadily but modestly to the end of the century but declined rapidly thereafter as the "imitators" he inspired began competing with him for the market. The foreshortening of his holdings augured ill for Blake. Financial reverses put the firm into receivership, and its creditors sold the business in 1806 to Boston bookbinder William Andrews.

Blake stayed on for a time in Boston at No.3 School Street, but he later betook himself to New York. In 1818 he was proprietor of a book and stationery store there at 249 Broadway, where he maintained also a small circulating library. Little is known about his New York operation except that his library collection there was surprisingly light in fiction and even more surprisingly heavy in religion and philosophy, the former comprising only 17 and the latter fully 25 percent of his total. William Blake, who had been born in Boston in 1769, died unmarried in New York in 1820 after almost thirty years as a keeper of circulating libraries in two cities. His major service, however, was clearly to the novel-readers of Boston where, during the 1790s he was probably that community's largest purveyor of fiction.

Hocquet Caritat.[20] The proprietor of the finest American circulating library in the eighteenth century—indeed perhaps ever—was an amazing French immigrant named Hocquet Caritat. Caritat was born on the banks of the Marne in 1752 and was pensioned out of the royal household thirty-six years later. When it became clear that his pension was jeopardized by political developments in France, Caritat sailed for America where from 1793 to 1795 he operated a modest circulating library in company with New York bookseller John Fellows. Returning to France, Caritat was chagrined to learn that he had lost his citizenship there and that his property had been forfeited to the Republic. Coming again to America in 1797—some say this time as a secret agent for the French government—Caritat bought out his old partner and opened anew at 93 Pearl Street, "a little below the Old Slip," with about 2,500 volumes.

This time Caritat expanded his operations very rapidly. In less than a year he claimed to have more than four thousand volumes, and before the end of 1800 his shelves—both sale and library—contained an astonishing thirty thousand volumes![21] Since subscribers to his library had the privilege of renting any books in the establishment, save for rare volumes or works of reference, they had borrowing access to more than twice as many books with Caritat than with any other library *of any kind*—circulating, social, public, or college—in America.

The quality of Caritat's library was at least as important as the size. Perhaps no library curator anywhere had taken greater pains to assure that his shelves contained the very best in recent literature. He scoured the European reviews and journals for the comments of critics and pored over booksellers' catalogues striving constantly to enhance his offerings to the public. From 1800 onward he was the American agent for William Lane's Minerva Press, England's largest publisher and circulating library of contemporary fiction.

Caritat not only brought together the largest library in America, but he also sought to have it used. His catalogues of 1799 and 1804 were not simple, brief listings of the books on his shelves arranged by size, as was contemporary practice. They were rather "explanatory" or annotated catalogues, numbering 215 and 322 pages respectively, arranged systematically by subject and containing fuller bibliographical detail than was common for the time. He published brief and long notes and essays extolling the social benefits of good fiction in an unabashed effort to make American readers less self-conscious about their heavy preference for novels. He developed and maintained a handsome noncirculating collection of bibliographical and reference works which he made available not only to his subscribers but to others as well.

The rapid growth of Caritat's operation forced him to move several times in a relatively short span, but he came eventually in 1802 to settle in the most select business district of the town—No. 1 City Hotel, at 123 Broadway between Thames and Cedar. He erected a "Sign of Fenelon's Head" over the entrance and outfitted special commodious quarters as a fashionable literary salon to which admittance required a separate subscription fee. It was stocked with reference books, current newspapers, and reviews; tastefully furnished with fine chairs, reading tables, and writing desks; provided with stationery and with coffee available; and kept open throughout the day "to ladies as well as gentlemen." Lectures and readings were scheduled in this so-called Literary Assembly. Although it became one of New York's most genteel resorts, this aspect of Caritat's operation failed within two years, owing in part to disagreement among its subscribers as to whether it was to be a quiet room or a conversation room but also in part to general lack of patronage. In many of its characteristics Caritat's Literary Assembly anticipated the Boston Athenaeum which was successfully established only three years later and which continues today.

Caritat was not satisfied to let business come to him; he also carried his business to readers. In 1803 he began dispatching his books to and from the sloops that sailed regularly to other towns in the New York vicinity where he had subscribers. He was able, because of his extensive collections and services, to command the highest rental rates of his time, amounting to Six Dollars annually for the right to borrow one volume or set at a time or Eight Dollars for two. He charged fines amounting to a penny a day for books kept overdue beyond ten days, the fines going to the Female Society for the Relief of Widows with Small Children.

Some say Caritat's health broke in 1804; others say he

completed his secret service to the French government at that time. Whichever the case may have been, in that year he sold his library and returned to France, where he was granted amnesty, his property was returned, and his pension was restored. In 1816, at age sixty-four, he appeared again in New York, but he was soon frustrated in his new aspiration to develop a mercantile agency. A year later he sold his assets there and virtually disappeared from view, apparently forever.

There is no question but that Hocquet Caritat left an indelible mark upon the city of New York and upon the field of American letters. One significant aspect of his influence is colorfully captured by John Davis, who knew him well.

> I would place the bust of Caritat among those of the *Sosii* of *Horace*, and the *Centryphon* of *Quintillian*. . . . His talents were not meanly cultivated by letters; he could tell a good book from a bad one, which few modern Librarians can do. But *place aux dames* was his maxim, and all the ladies of *New-York* declared that the Library of Mr. *Caritat* was charming. . . . Novels were called for by the young and the old; from the tender virgin of thirteen, whose little heart went pit-a-pat at the approach of a beau; to the experienced matron of three score, who could not read without spectacles.[22]

Caritat, however, influenced the reading and literary taste of men as well as women, giving to many the self-confidence to abide with impunity by their predilections. He pioneered in the frank encouragement of an Amercian literati whilst also bringing to a very large American reading public the best of Europe's books and journals. He created the largest library in the Western Hemisphere and promoted widespread awareness of the social and cultural role of books. Most astonishing of all perhaps is the fact that he attained these manifold accomplishments in the brief compass of only eight years.

Summary

Americans read even more following the Revolution than they had before it, with the greatest increases being made in the field of current affairs and especially in fiction. Circulating library proprietors redoubled their efforts to meet the need for this additional literature by enlarging their holdings, increasing the representation of novels on their shelves, opening additional establishments in new locations, making them more easily accessible, and catering where needed to foreign-speaking populations. By the turn of the century several circulating libraries had become major cultural forces in their communities, with Hocquet Caritat's operation in New York earning the distinction of being the largest library to that time in America.

REFERENCES

1. Jesse H. Shera, *Foundations of the Public Library* (Chicago: University of Chicago Press, 1949), pp. 55, 69.
2. Hellmut Lehmann-Haupt, *The Book in America* (N.Y.: R. R. Bowker, 1939), p. 102.
3. *Bibliotheca Americana; or A Chronological Catalogue of the Most Curious and Interesting Books, Pamphlets, State Papers, &c. upon the Subject of North and South America* (London: J. Debrett, 1789), pp. 16-17.
4. A copy of Larkin's catalogue is preserved in the American Antiquarian Society.
5. *Georgia Gazette*, January 26, 1798; *Savannah Columbian Museum*, April 26, 1799.
6. *Pittsburgh Gazette*, July 26, 1788.
7. Louis B. Wright, *Culture on the Moving Frontier* (N.Y.: Harper, 1955), p. 84.
8. *Pittsburgh Gazette*, December 22, 29, 1798. Merchants had

apparently lent books earlier in Pittsburgh, however. One store-keeper who advertised "many hundreds of volumes on divinity, history, voyages, &c. for sale" (ibid., April 11, 1789) later called for the return of those he had lent so he could auction them off (ibid., January 30, 1790).

9. "Note" *Pennsylvania Magazine of History and Biography* 24 (1900): 526; *Philadelphia Aurora*, January 1, 1799.

10. James Owen Knauss, Jr. *Social Conditions among the Pennsylvania Germans in the Eighteenth Century* (Lancaster: Pennsylvania-German Society, 1922), p. 102.

11. *Der Lancaster Correspondent*, January 25, July 12, 1800.

12. Marcus Lee Hanson, *The Atlantic Migration, 1607-1860*. (N.Y.: Harper, 1961), p. 58.

13. *Philadelphia Aurora*, December 8, 1797; May 30, 1798; November 4, 1799.

14. John Dabney's establishment has already been well reported by Harriet S. Tapley in her *Salem Imprints, 1768-1825* (Salem, Mass.: The Essex Institute, 1927), pp. 172-76, to which the present author is greatly indebted.

15. Ibid., p. 173.

16. Quoted ibid., p. 176.

17. October 23, 1819.

18. Much of the following material regarding Blake is adapted from Charles K. Bolton's "Circulating Libraries in Boston, 1765-1865," *Publications of the Colonial Society of Massachusetts* 11 (February 1907): 201-03.

19. Ibid.

20. Hocquet Caritat has perhaps been more thoroughly studied than any other circulating library proprietor in America, all by George Gates Raddin. See his *Hocquet Caritat and the Early New York Literary Scene* (Dover, N.J.: Dover Advance Press, 1953); *An Early New York Library of Fiction* (N.Y.: H. W. Wilson, 1940); *Caritat and the Genet Episode* (Dover, N.J.: Dover Advance Press, 1953); and *The New York of Hocquet Caritat and His Associates* (Dover, N.J.: Dover Advance Press, 1953). The present summary of Caritat's life and library is drawn largely from those sources.

21. Raddin, *Hocquet Caritat*, p. 30.

22. John Davis, *Travels of Four Years and a Half in the United States of America* (Bristol: E. Edwards, 1803), pp. 186-87.

Chapter Four
Maturity, from 1800 to 1850

The first half of the nineteenth century was the heyday of the circulating library in America. The motivation to read held strong throughout the period, but free public library service was not yet generally available to meet its needs, and commercial library service was competitively priced with the social subscription libraries. The population of the nation increased more than fourfold during the period, with much of it going to the new towns in the Northwest Territory, the Old Southwest, and beyond. When the century began, the center of population in the United States was in the middle of Maryland; by midcentury it was in central Ohio. The mercantile instinct was, as always, quick to sense these new markets, and bookmen along with other traders followed hard on the heels of the migrants, opening stands in the new communities. Circulating libraries, usually still associated with other enterprises, were established widely to provide reading material, now even more predominantly fiction than before, to readers who desired an alternative to purchasing. With a single major exception, few important changes were adopted in circulating library technique during this time; for the most part they pursued practices that had been tested and proved before the century began.

Popular Preferences in Literature

Popular reading in America during the first half of the nineteenth century continued in the same course that it had followed since the Revolution. Remaining at the top of the public preference was the newspaper, the prime carrier of information necessary for widespread participation in the democratic process, especially following the extension of suffrage in the Jacksonian period. Foreign visitors especially found the extent of newspaper reading by Americans almost incomprehensible. In her usual acerb fashion, Mrs. Trollope allowed that newspapers were so popular because they catered to the lowest common denominator in the nation's literary taste. She also felt, with some reason, that the extensive reading of newspapers impeded the development of a native American literature.[1] Maximilian, Prince of Wied, with predictable aristocratic myopia, saw but failed to recognize the motivation behind American newspaper reading when he wrote somewhat quizzically of the gentlemen

> whom you see all the day long posted before the inns [in the U.S.], or at the fire-side in the lower rooms, smoking cigars and reading the colossal newspapers. . . . "Elegance of dress" is all that the gentleman in America cares about, when he has finished his mercantile business, read the newspaper, *and performed his part in the government of the State [italics added]*.[2]

To meet this need for the dissemination of information requisite to exercising the popular franchise, the number of newspapers being produced in the nation rose dramatically. There had been some 220 newspapers in 1800, many of which were short-lived and of limited patronage, and only about fifteen of which were dailies. By midcentury, however, fully 254 newspapers were appearing daily, and there were countless other weekly, bi-weekly, and tri-weekly papers as well. It has been estimated that some 13 million copies of newspapers were produced in the United States in 1800, or about 2½ copies per capita per year, whereas by midcentury the daily papers alone were producing ten copies per year for every inhabitant.[3]

Beyond newspapers, the most popular reading matter among early nineteenth-century Americans continued to be fiction. Where it had constituted less than 2 percent of the American book production in 1800, the composition by 1835 had increased to 15 percent. There were, however, two major changes in American novel reading during this time. First, a few key authors came to enjoy phenomenal popularity vastly greater than had been seen anywhere before; and second, whereas Americans had been reading English novelists almost exclusively in 1800, by a half century later native American authors were providing an estimated three-quarters of the novels coming from the nation's presses.[4]

The author to accrue greatest fame as a novelist was, of course, Sir Walter Scott. The lays and minstrels of the so-called "Wizard Harp of the North," were already widely read in America before his first novel *Waverley* appeared anonymously in 1814. Thereafter for decades his thirty-two novels were voraciously devoured by hundreds of thousands of Americans from the urbane east to the threshold of the savage frontier itself. One English traveller to Missouri in 1822 reported that Scott's novels could be had there within two months of their publication in England,[5] thanks in part to the alacrity of American reprinters in obtaining early proofsheets from Scott's Edinburgh publisher.[6]

Scott's popularity, together with innovations designed by publishers to serve it, paved the way for other novelists of consummate skill to gain extremely wide readership also. Thus when James Fenimore Cooper betook his wares to the Philadelphia house of Carey & Lea in 1826, his fame and fortune suddenly abounded as that firm pumped copies in huge quantities to avid readers from cabin to plantation in the country and from garret to mansion in the towns.[7] Likewise the works of Charles Dickens, following 1837, found immediate and extensive favor among the nation's readers of fiction.

Again, however, to dwell upon the few greatest novelists and to ignore the many other literary craftsmen whose works were also read, albeit in lesser numbers, would be to distort the actual scene. Other American novelists had their followings. John Pendleton Kennedy's *Swallow Barn* (1832) and *Horse Shoe Robinson* (1834) attained recognition, as did also physician Robert Montgomery Bird with his *Calavar* (1832), *The Hawks of Hawk Hollow* (1835), *The Infidel* (1835), and his best book *Nick of the Woods* (1837). Southern novelist William Gilmore Simms' first novel *Guy Rivers* was tagged a hit immediately upon its appearance in 1834, and he produced many other widely-read stories, both before and after midcentury. Among British novelists who enjoyed large followings in America during this time were Edward Bulwer-Lytton, the Brontës, William M. Thackeray, and Frederick Marryatt, as well as Irish story-tellers Samuel Lover and Charles Lever. There continued also throughout this period to be a hefty flow of other novels and tales, many anonymous or pseudonymous, which were widely read but appear to have made little permanent impression upon the nation's literary inheritance.

The historical novel especially was avidly sought, but it did not by itself fill the desire by American readers for books about the past. Writers of history *per se* also enjoyed large markets during this time. William Robertson's *History of Scotland*, written before the Revolution but not reprinted in the United States until 1811, was standard reading fare, as were also Henry Trumbull's *History of the Discovery of America* and later Thomas Babington Macaulay's *History of England*. Prime position in this category, of course, belongs to Washington

Irving, whose *History of New York, Conquest of Granada, Astoria,* and other historical works were extremely popular.

America's historical interest manifested itself also in the large number of biographies and memoirs which were read during this period. Best-seller when the century opened was *The Life of Washington* by the fascinating sometime clergyman, peddler, author, and master of the *bon mot* Mason Locke Weems. This not-too-faithful presentation went through more than thirty editions before midcentury and accounts for some of the nation's most cherished anecdota about its first President. Scott's *Life of Napoleon* in 1827, and John Gibson Lockhart's *Memoirs of the Life of Sir Walter Scott* a decade later both set sales records. Especially welcome to readers were lives of individuals who had brushed with the American frontier. The autobiography of Mary Jemison, who had lived in captivity among the Delawares for some three score years and ten, was much sought following its appearance in 1824. The Jacksonian ascendency brought with it interest in such works concerning the "Western Country" as the autobiographical *Narrative of the Life of David Crockett* (1834) and Timothy Flint's *Daniel Boone* (1833). All in all, through histories, biographies, and historical novels, American readers kept themselves well apprised of their heritage during this half-century period.

Effect on Circulating Libraries

In accord with good principles of merchandising, the circulating libraries between 1800 and 1850 trimmed their collections promptly to conform to these changes in popular taste. Through the first half of the period the representation of fiction among their holdings continued the steady rise it had sustained from the beginning. Whereas fiction appears to have comprised about a fourth of the bookstock of the "typical" pre-War circulating library, it had risen by 1820 to more than half. Thereafter, however, it seems to have held approximately level until after mid-century. Books of history, biography, and travel maintained a firm grip on their share of shelf space. Following 1820, however, books on philosophy and religion found their numbers dwindling, except in the few libraries that catered especially to those interests, such as Joseph Buckingham's and John Creery's theological libraries in Boston and Baltimore respectively and Bernard Dornin's ill-starred "Roman Catholic Library" also in the latter city.[8] Poetry, essays, and plays seem to have enjoyed a steady readership to about 1830 but to have declined somewhat sharply in popularity thereafter.

In terms of size, no other American circulating libraries during the period from 1800 to 1850 seem to have developed collections as large as Caritat's. The well-stocked, major establishments of some permanence in the larger cities sustained libraries ranging between 1,500 and 3,000 titles (perhaps 3,000 to 6,000 volumes), with a few smaller and a few larger. This appears to have been an optimal size under normal conditions. The large number of small, short-lived circulating libraries established during the time in the villages and lesser towns tended to depress considerably the average or median size of their collections.

The number of new circulating libraries being established rose rapidly as the nineteenth century began. Whereas 9 new libraries had opened in the five-year period from 1790 to 1794 and 12 additional ones had come into being between 1795 and 1799, the first five years of the new century saw at least 27 new institutions, and even larger numbers were posted in each subsequent five-year period until 1825. Many of these new libraries were in the country beyond the Alleghenies. Following the rivers, reading matter within the first quarter of the nineteenth century was available for rent in Ohio, Indiana, Kentucky, Missouri, and Louisiana. By 1850 there was a circulating library in Colorado.

Although the principal locus for circulating libraries continued to be the bookstores, many were located in other kinds of establishments as well. Not infrequently they were operated by women or were situated in locations women might be expected to frequent. For more than two decades Keziah Butler maintained a circulating library in conjunction with her milliner's shop in Boston. From 1802 to 1806 Mary Sprague of Boston operated a library in her millinery store as well. Miss Sprague, who advertised caps, turbans, muslins, Grecian robes, fancy and staple goods, as well as mantua-making, invited the patronage of gentlemen as well as ladies and stressed the fact that her library contained nonfiction as well as fiction.

> She has spared no pains to make her collection deserving circulation [she announced in the third person], by mingling the useful with the amusing. In selecting volumes, she has not confined her choices to Romances and Magazines—Philosophy, History, Biography, valuable Travels, useful Miscellany, Moral Essays, the various productions of the Muses, and whatever instructs while it pleases, have portions of the shelves allotted to them. The newest productions will always be procured by first opportunities; & as the Library will be calculated for Ladies as well as Gentlemen, she flatters herself she shall receive the patronage of her Sex.[9]

The Misses Butler and Sprague were not without competition from others of their sex, however, as Caroline Fanning and Lydia Reed were also both in the library business there during the same period. Also in Boston the Ladies Circulating Library, maintained by

N. Nutting, flourished throughout the 1820s at 45½ Newbury Street. Its 66-page catalogue produced in 1829 is the only extant catalogue from the period of a library which was avowedly oriented to a female clientele. It reveals a large bookstock of more than 2,300 titles, of which almost two-thirds were novels. It is curious to note that although the first 21 pages of this catalogue are meticulously organized, first by broad classification and then alphabetically, pages 22 through 66 represent a total contrast, with titles arranged solely by arbitrary shelf numbers and without index. It is difficult to see how the latter portion of this catalogue served either proprietor or patron.

Boston was not the only city with libraries operated by women. Hannah Harris is reported to have stocked some 4,000 volumes in her Central Circulating Library in Salem during the early 1820s. "The Widow Bradish" was maintaining a library at 124 Broadway in New York in 1811, as was "the Widow Roche" in New Orleans in the same year. For a quarter century beginning in 1821 a Miss Jordan operated a library in Lancaster about which little other information has come to light. A Mrs. Richardson conducted the Minerva Circulating Library [a branch of the enterprise in England by the same name?][10] along with her "Ladies Academy" in Providence in 1809, and Lucy Hunter continued William Munday's Baltimore Circulating Library for many years after his death in 1819. In Philadelphia from 1814 to 1820 Christina Neale kept a library in her bookstore on Chestnut Street adjacent to the New Theatre at the same time that Ann Shallus, with her "Circulating Library and Fancy Goods Store," was located at 90 South Third. Ann Shallus then removed to New Orleans where she opened a similar establishment in 1822.

Not all circulating libraries, by any means, were situated in locations where only women might be expected

CATALOGUE OF BOOKS

IN THE

Louisville Circulating Library,

CONSISTING OF

HISTORIES, BIOGRAPHIES, NOVELS, TALES, ECCLESI-
ASTICAL, PHRENOLOGICAL, AND A GREAT
VARIETY OF MISCELLANEOUS WORKS

IN

EVERY DEPARTMENT OF LITERATURE.

LOUISVILLE, KY.

W. N. HALDEMAN,
LITERARY DEPOT, FOURTH-ST.

1842.

Title Page of the Catalogue of the Louisville Circulating Library,
1842 (Orig. 7½ x 4½ inches).

to go. Travellers, male and female, had access to the circulating libraries aboard the river boats on the Mississippi,[11] the barges on the Erie Canal (where Mrs. Trollope experienced a "library of a dozen books" between Utica and Schenectady in 1831),[12] and the packets plying Long Island Sound and the Hudson River (which sometimes boasted libraries of five hundred volumes).[13] Women, perhaps more so than men, would frequent the music stores of George Blake in Philadelphia and of Nathan S. Parkhurst in Providence, as well as Matthew Davenport's fabric shop in Cumberland, Rhode Island, where the proprietors also kept libraries. They might with impunity visit Thomas Porter's soda fountain in Salem, or John Cook's Albany outlet for Saratoga Spring water, or Dr. Powell's office in Boston, where circulating libraries could also be consulted. It seems less likely, however, that they would be regular customers of Solon Robinson, auctioneer of Madison, Indiana; William Yearnshaw, employment and real estate counselor of Woonsocket, Rhode Island; Adams Foster, coal dealer of Providence; Z. Ernst & Son, brewers of Cincinnati; B. Taylor, surveyor of New York; or of Silas Marchant's lottery office in Pawtucket, all of whom also maintained circulating libraries or subscription reading rooms. Regrettably, evidence concerning the composition of the book collections in these diverse locations is too scanty to permit inferences or even speculation to be made concerning them. Good librarians, however, have always attempted to meet the specific needs of their unique clientele, and these may be presumed to have done so as well.

Subscription Reading Rooms

The most significant innovation perhaps ever to come into circulating library practice appeared during this time. It was the privately-owned subscription reading room. Prior to 1800 few libraries of any kind in America provided areas in which patrons could read the books they contained. Libraries were generally thought to be collections of books and nothing more.

As was mentioned at the opening of this study, eighteenth-century coffeehouses usually kept a very limited range of reading material—gazettes and prices-current from the surrounding towns and sometimes even from afar—which patrons were welcome to consult as they drank their coffee. There had long been an affinity between coffeehouses and printing office/bookstores; often they operated in the same building and under the same proprietorship. In a sense, the coffeehouses provided the earliest public reading facilities in America.[14]

By the turn of the century, however, a number of trends and events had begun to coalesce to force a greater degree of formality upon these incipient reading rooms. The rising need for current information regarding social and political affairs was spurring increased reading of newspapers. Commerce and trade were increasingly requiring currency of information regarding market conditions, commodity prices, and other mercantile intelligences, again prompting greater attention to newspapers. Legislative actions affecting the life and work of citizens were not considered fully consummated until resulting new laws had been promulgated through their publication in the newspapers. The time was also one of constant motion in society, as the frontier drew veritable migrations of people from place to place, creating unprecedented interest in the most recent dispatches of all kinds from elsewhere.

The Congress, in recognition of this need for a free flow of information of all kinds among the states and territories, adopted a key provision in the Postal Law of February 20, 1792. This provision allowed any printer of an American newspaper to frank single copies of his paper to each and every other newspaper printer in the nation.[15] This early subsidy of the newspaper industry by the federal government, conceived to be in the national interest, facilitated the exchange of papers among their proprietors and provided for their columns the main source of news from other communities. Many printers exchanged their papers under this franking privilege with as many as fifty, seventy-five, and even a hundred printers elsewhere.

It was these newspapers received on exchange that were the reading matter in the local coffeehouses of the late eighteenth century. If the proprietor were not himself a printer, he arranged with the local printing office to keep its files of papers on hand for the patrons of his establishment after the local editor had gleaned his copy from them. As long as coffee-selling was brisk and the number of newspapers relatively small, this was an easy service to maintain. Understandably, however, as the number of papers being exchanged increased, and as the mobility and information needs of the populace grew, the administration of the free reading-room service became burdensome. By 1800 some had come to believe that reading facilities, to be properly appointed and attended, would require special provision.

It is not known just who established the first separately administered reading room in the United States. Aarondt Van Hook opened a small *non*-circulating library and reading room on Water Street in New York in 1797, but he died in the yellow fever epidemic a year later, and his establishment collapsed.[16] G. Painter proposed opening a reading room in New York in 1798, but little is known of it.[17] Caritat's Literary Assembly had many of the characteristics of the proprietary reading room, but it appears to have been much more oriented to letters than to trade.

Subscription reading rooms appear to have become important earliest in the Western Country. Perhaps the most elaborate such resort was that operated in Lexington, Kentucky, by a Mr. Terasse. A visitor to the place in 1807 described it as follows:

> There is a coffee house here, where is a reading room for the benefit of subscribers and strangers, in which are forty-two files of different newspapers from various parts of the United States. It is supported by subscribers, who pay six dollars each annually, and of which there are now sixty. In the same house is a billiard table, and chess and backgammon tables, and the guests may be accommodated with wine, porter, beer, spirituous liquors, cordials, and confectionary. . . . Mr. Terasse has opened a little publick garden behind his house, which he calls Vauxhall. It has a most luxuriant grape arbour, and two or three summer houses, formed also of grape vines, all of which are illuminated with variegated lamps, every Wednesday evening, when the musick of two or three decent performers sometimes excites parties to dance on a small boarded platform in the middle of the arbour. It is becoming a place of fashionable resort.[18]

It would be interesting to know whence came Mr. Terasse's newspaper files. Almost certainly they had been received on exchange by a Lexington printing office.

In the same year Joseph Charless, proprietor of the *Louisville Gazette*, proposed to open a coffeehouse and reading room in Louisville, where he would make available the fifty or so newspaper files that he received on exchange. The establishment would be open from 9 AM to 9 PM in winter and from 8 AM to 10 PM in summer. Access to the facility would be by subscription at Eight Dollars per year. It is not known if he ever carried out his scheme, however. Charless may have opened the first trans-Mississippi reading room a year later when he removed to St. Louis in 1808 to establish the *Missouri Gazette* and a bookstore there. He also advertised the availability of "refreshments," and he later opened a hotel.[19] That he maintained a reading room may be inferred, and a mental image of it conjured from an anecdote recorded by the Scots naturalist John Bradbury in 1810. Bradbury told of visiting an Omaha village some five hundred miles northwest of St. Louis where two Indians approached him indicating that they had seen him before.

> I had no recollection of these Indians [he wrote] but they pointed down the river to St. Louis; afterwards they took up the corner of the buffalo robe, held it before their faces, and turned it over as a man does a newspaper in reading it. This action will be explained by relating that I frequented the printing-office of Mr. Joseph Charless, when in St. Louis, to read the papers from the United States, when it often happened that the Indians at the place on business came into the office and sat down. Mr. Charless, out of pleasantry, would hand to each a newspaper, which, out of respect for the custom of the whites, they examined with as much attention as if they could read it, turning it over at the same time that they saw me turn that with which I was engaged.[20]

A similar subscription reading room, stocked with "periodicals, pamphlets, price currents, and newspapers," was maintained by Elihu Stout in his Vincennes printing office, the first in the Indiana Territory, in 1814.[21] Thereafter until midcentury they comprised a common adjunct to newspaper establishments throughout the country.

Subscription reading rooms, operated for profit and specializing in current newspapers and recent journals, were also to be found conjoined to many other kinds of businesses, including hotels, taverns, bookstores, milliners' shops, soda fountains, breweries, and merchants' exchanges. A few operated standing apart from other enterprises, such as Stephen G. Benedict's Pawtucket Reading Room which he opened in the Post Office there in 1832. Benedict, who claimed to have about fifty "gentlemen" who had subscribed his operation at Two Dollars per year, strove to stock "the best newspapers and pamphlets in the country." He viewed his enterprise as only a temporary venture, however, and announced that "until a regular village library is established, a good supply of books will be located in the room, for the use of subscribers."[22]

Reading Rooms in Circulating Libraries

Not infrequently subscription reading rooms came to be added to circulating libraries. It was abundantly clear that some kinds of reading material—especially the kind then ascending most rapidly in popularity (*e.g.*, current newspapers, journals, and pamphlets)—did not really lend themselves well to the conventional lending practices of the circulating libraries, yet the circulating libraries had to stock them. Such ephemeral materials lost their readership very quickly—("Pamphlets, when a few days old," observed Mathew Carey in 1809, "are the veriest Wrath that can Be")[23]—and they needed to be kept on hand where they could see quick turnover and suffer prompt withdrawal rather than be lent out for up to a month. The circulating libraries soon came to realize that the subscription reading room was a much more effective way of providing access to such publications.

It is not possible to say just when the merging of the two kinds of activities began, as it seems reasonable to assume that some reading has always gone on in libraries. Charging nonmembers for on-site reading was probably begun early to discourage excessive lounging. Indeed Pierre Roche [husband of the later "Widow Roche" of New Orleans?], who kept a circulating library of primarily French works in Baltimore in 1804, seems to have reversed the standard procedure of charging for borrowing and concentrated his charges on reading instead. He advertised that his terms were One Dollar per month "for persons who read at the room in the day. Persons desiring to take the books to their own houses, will please to deposit two dollars, that will be returned" when the books are returned.[24] This may have been rather like Van Hook's "standing library" in New York six years earlier.

One of the more elaborate commercial reading establishments of the period was run in conjunction with one of the stronger circulating libraries. In 1809 Joseph Robinson, printer-bookseller of Baltimore, proposed opening a "New Circulating Library and Reading Room" with access to the library costing Five Dollars per year and the reading room costing Three.[25] Although Robinson's library was in full operation by 1812,[26] nothing more is heard of his plan for a reading room until 1818 by which time his "Literary Rooms" were available at Four Dollars annually above the library fee of Six Dollars.[27]

Robinson's establishment, which was located in 1822 at the corner of Market and Belvidere Streets, comprised four public rooms. The main reception and book delivery room was on the first floor, and the proprietor requested that men not congregate or socialize there because, as he explained "a great proportion of the patrons of the Library are ladies." The room adjacent was for the sole use of women; it contained in addition to reading tables and writing desks "a Piano Forte for the purpose of trying Music." The two upstairs rooms were habituated apparently only by men. One was a quiet room for reading and study, and the other, where conversation was allowed, was where the newspapers were kept.[28]

Robinson's book collection contained some 6,000 volumes when it was opened,[29] and at first it grew slowly. In 1816 Robinson published a catalogue of his holdings, listing more than 2,200 titles, more than three-quarters of which were fiction and *belles-lettres*. He issued supplemental catalogues in 1816, 1818, and 1819. In 1823 Robinson purchased the circulating library of George Blake of Philadelphia and merged it with his own; thereafter he claimed his 15,000 volumes to be "the most valuable and extensive reading collection in the country."[30]

In 1834, following the removal of his operation to No.2 North Calvert Street, Robinson altered his Literary Rooms so as to allow male visitors easier access to the gallery without obtruding themselves upon female patrons.[31] By 1842 Robinson's circulating library and reading rooms appear to have closed, but they had served as a fashionable literary resort for the residents of Baltimore for more than three decades.

Meanwhile bookbinder Samuel H. Parker had also opened a circulating library and reading room in Boston. In 1811 Parker took over the Union Circulating Library[32] that had been established fifteen years earlier by William Pelham and had been operated more recently by Pelham's nephew William Blagrove.[33] It was the largest circulating library in Boston when Parker assumed its proprietorship, and it retained that distinction for more than two decades thereafter.

In 1814 Parker moved the Union Circulating Library to more spacious quarters at No.4 Cornhill "at the head of Water-Street," where he added a reading room to his operation. "The Reading Room," he advised, "will be furnished with the principal Newspaper and Periodical Works published in the United States and of the Pamphlets of the day." Parker charged Seven Dollars per annum for access to his library plus Three Dollars additional for use of the reading room. The reading room alone, plus on-site use only of library books, cost Five Dollars per year.[34] His establishment remained open daily from 9 AM to 9 PM.

The Union Circulating Library book collection grew apace under Parker's supervision. His 1812 catalogue listed some 1,445 titles. His 1815 catalogue itemized about 2,260, and his 1820 catalogue contained approximately 3,435 titles, which translated to about 8,000 volumes. Between half and two-thirds of his books were novels, and he kept a good supply of plays, French books, general literature, history, books of travel, and biographies and memoirs, plus a small representation of standard titles in philosophy and religion, political economy, and science.

In 1820 Parker relocated his business down the street at No.12 Cornhill and in 1825 to No.164 Washington Street,[35] where he also sold stationery, "fancy goods," and music. He appears to have relinquished his library in 1833.[36]

During much of this same period Charles Callendar of Boston was also keeping a reading room in conjunction with his circulating library. In 1815 Callendar purchased the remnants of the old Boston Circulating Library, which had been established in 1787 by Benjamin Guild and had suffered many vicissitudes in the intervening years. In 1813, while in custody of bookseller Charles Metcalf, this library had taken on the style of "The Shakspeare Circulating Library," and it suited Callendar to retain that name when he took it over two years later.[37]

Callendar's collections seem somewhat atypical for his

time. Although his first catalogue, issued in 1815, depicts holdings very like those of the contemporary Union Circulating Library in size and scope, his second catalogue, published four years later, shows that he had by that time modified his shelf stock rather considerably. Overall he had foreshortened his holdings by about fifteen percent, and he had cut his representation of fiction by half while adding rather extensively to his literature holdings. This change occurred as a result of his auctioning off of his old collection in late 1818 and the subsequent replenishing of his stock in June of the following year.[38] Callendar's 1820 catalogue was in reality only his 1819 catalogue with a new wrapper; the body itself of the catalogue was not reset.

In 1816 Callendar removed his Shakspeare Circulating Library to larger quarters at No.25 School-Street at the corner of City Hall Avenue, where he also opened a reading room. Patrons of the reading room, who were assessed Five Dollars per year for the privilege, could use in the room any books from the library, and the proprietor kept on hand "the Papers of the Day, Portfolio, Analect Magazine, Edinburg [sic] and Quarterly Reviews, Pamphlets, and all other new Publications."[39] The privilege of borrowing books from the library cost an additional Seven Dollars per year for four volumes at a time. Nonsubscribers, however, could rent duodecimos, when they were not needed by members, for 6¼ Cents weekly; octavos or larger cost 12½ Cents.

Charles Callendar served the bookish needs of many Bostonians over a long period of time. Although he died about 1840, his wife and son continued the library for at least fifteen years thereafter. Callendar was described as "very near-sighted . . . [and] eccentric. He dressed and posed for Shakespeare, and was a well-read man. The whole institution was as Boston as the Old South and baked beans."[40] Following his death, a patron of the Shakspeare Circulating Library wrote:

. . . to find a more liberal, genial, obliging librarian than Mr. Callendar would be very difficult. He was a devoted admirer and constant reader of Shakspeare. His giving the name of the great poet to his library was not a clap-trap in trade, but a sincere, genuine expression of his love and veneration for the author. . . . The intimate friends of Mr. Callendar claimed that it was impossible for an exigence in the tide of human affairs to turn up which he cou'd not meet with an appropriate, close-fitting quotation from Shakspeare.[41]

Perhaps the most interesting reading room proprietor of all, however, was the New Orleans milliner, bookseller, and savante, Mary Carroll. This fascinating woman, who has suffered undeserved neglect at the hands of latter-day scholars, had emigrated alone from her native Ireland at the tender age of fourteen[42] to become one of the leading literati of the Louisiana town. Her business establishment became the center of intellectual and literary ferment, and she was befriended and admired by such utopians and freethinkers as Robert Owen, Frances Wright, and other radical reformers of her time. Although she claimed to be "a coward at heart," she was a woman with a mind of her own, not easily daunted by the will of others or the weight of circumstances arrayed against her. She willingly risked ostracism and loss of much-needed business by admitting publicly to her preference for unpopular liberal causes, but at the same time she chided her friend Frances Wright, in a series of beautifully-written letters, for what she felt was the latter's unnecessarily strident advertising of her radical opinions.[43]

Even Frances Trollope liked Mary Carroll.

I was told [she wrote],·that she possessed great intellectual endowments, and much information; I really believe this was true. Her manner was easy and graceful, with a good deal of French tournure; and the gentleness with which her fine eyes and sweet voice directed the movements of a young female slave, was really touching: the way too in which she blended her French talk of modes with her customers, and her English talk of metaphysics with her friends, had a pretty air of indifference in it, that gave her a superiority with both.[44]

Mary Carroll's reading room was in operation by 1830,[45] and although it served a useful function in New Orleans for several years, it never really thrived as she felt it should. At best she was able to attract the patronage of only about fifty subscribers, although her collection of reading matter appears to have been quite good. A visitor to her establishment about 1832 described her stock as

> consisting of the American and British Reviews,—the Libraries of Useful and Entertaining Knowledge,— the New York and other American newspapers,—a few magazines, political and religious,—with only one British newspaper, which, I was surprised and pleased to find, was the Scotsman of Edinburgh,—a paper which has uniformly maintained a high character, not only for talent, but for the consistency and constitutional soundness of the political opinions which it has advocated. Miss Carrol told me that . . . she could not afford a British daily paper, and had got the Scotsman, because it was recommended to her as the best of the twice a-week papers.[46]

That may have been, but also Mary Carroll was Irish, and it has never been easy for the Irish to patronize an English newspaper.

This intrepid reading room proprietor died in the cholera epidemic of 1833 leaving an impact upon the

New Orleans literary ambience which was of considerable consequence but apparently only gently felt.

Summary

The first half of the nineteenth century saw the American circulating library at its zenith. Reading was widespread among the populace, and newspapers and novels especially seem never to have been available in adequate numbers to sate the public's desire for them. Circulating libraries grew in number, and the representation of fiction increased upon their shelves, as their proprietors sought to meet the demand for novels. The popular demand for current literature, including newspapers and journals, encouraged entrepreneurs also to provide reading establishments to which the public could subscribe and where such current publications could be perused. Many circulating libraries added subscription reading rooms to their operations so as to facilitate public access not only to their books but also to their lesser and more ephemeral holdings. The better of these establishments sometimes made substantive contributions to the literary and intellectual lives of the communities in which they were located.

REFERENCES

1. Frances Trollope, *Domestic Manners of the Americans* (N.Y.: Knopf, 1974), pp. 82-83.
2. Maximilian, Prince of Wied, *Travels in the Interior of North America* (London: Ackerman, 1843), p. 5.
3. Samuel Miller, *Brief Retrospect of the Eighteenth Century*, 2 vols. (N.Y.: T. J. Swords, 1803), 2: 251; U.S. Bureau of the Census, *A Century of Population Growth* (Washington: Government Printing Office, 1909), p. 25.
4. S. G. Goodrich, *Recollections of a Lifetime*, 2 vols. (N.Y.: Miller, Orton and Mulligan, 1856), 2: 389.

5. William Blane, *Excursion through the United States and Canada* (London: Baldwin, 1824), p. 196.

6. David Kaser, "Waverley in America," *Papers of the Bibliographical Society of America* 5 (1957): 163-67.

7. David Kaser, *Messrs. Carey & Lea of Philadelphia* (Philadelphia: University of Pennsylvania Press, 1957), pp. 79-82.

8. David Kaser, "Bernard Dornin, America's First Catholic Bookseller," *Books in America's Past* (Charlottesville: University Press of Virginia, 1966), pp. 105-28.

9. *Boston Independent Chronicle*, May 17, 1802; *Boston Columbian Centinel*, May 22, 1802.

10. Dorothy Blakey, *The Minerva Press, 1790-1820* (London: Bibliographical Society, 1939).

11. W. Bullock, *Sketch of a Journey through the Western States of North America* (London: John Miller, 1827), p. xii.

12. Trollope, *Domestic Manners*, p. 272.

13. Harry Skallerup, *Books Afloat & Ashore* (Hamden, Conn.: Archon, 1974), p. 47.

14. David Kaser, "Coffee House to Stock Exchange: A Natural History of the Reading Room," *Milestones to the Present; Papers from Library History Seminar V* (Syracuse: Gaylord Professional Publications, 1978), pp. 238-54.

15. Second Congress. Session I. Ch. 7. Sec. 21. 1792.

16. George Gates Raddin, *Hocquet Caritat and the Early New York Literary Scene* (Dover, N.J.: Dover Advance Press, 1953), pp. 27, 127.

17. C. Seymour Thompson, *Evolution of the American Public Library, 1653-1876* (Washington, D.C.: Scarecrow, 1952), pp. 67-68.

18. Fortescue Cuming, *Sketches of a Tour to the Western Country* (Pittsburgh: Cramer, Spear & Eichbaum, 1810), pp. 166-67.

19. David Kaser, *Joseph Charless, Printer in the Western Country* (Philadelphia: University of Pennsylvania Press, 1963), pp. 132-34.

20. John Bradbury, *Travels in the Interior of America* (London: Sherwood, Neely, and Jones, 1819), p. 76n.

21. Jacob Piatt Dunn, *Libraries of Indiana* (Indianapolis: W. B. Burford, 1893).

22. *Pawtucket Chronicle*, February 17, 1832.

23. A.L.S., dated May 18, 1809, to Bernard Dornin. Carey Letter Books in the Historical Society of Pennsylvania.

24. *Baltimore Federal Gazette*, October 13, 1804.

25. *Baltimore American*, July 20, 1809.

26. Ibid., May 30, 1812.

27. *Baltimore Federal Gazette*, May 14, 1818.

28. *Baltimore American*, November 1, 1822; see also ibid., September 18, 1822.

29. *Baltimore Federal Gazette*, November 19, 1812.

30. *Baltimore American*, April 15, 1823.

31. *Baltimore Gazette and Daily Advertiser*, April 17, 1834.

32. *Boston Columbian Centinel*, April 27, 1811.

33. Charles K. Bolton, "Circulating Libraries in Boston, 1765-1865," *Publications of the Colonial Society of Massachusetts* 11 (February 1907): 204.

34. *Boston Columbian Centinel*, August 24, 1814.

35. Rollo G. Silver, *The Boston Book Trade, 1800-1825* (N.Y.: New York Public Library, 1949), p. 38.

36. Bolton, "Circulating Libraries," 204n.

37. *Boston Columbian Centinel*, August 8, 1810; August 26, 1812; March 31, 1813; *Boston Independent Chronicle*, July 17, 1815. Callendar may, however, have contemplated changing the name of the establishment when he took it over. Some indecision regarding the name, at any rate, may be inferred from Callendar's first catalogue, which was issued in 1815. Although the title-page reads "New Circulating Library," the running title and the conditions of subscription are for the "Shakspeare Circulating Library."

38. Ibid., October 17, 1818; *Boston Columbian Centinel*, June 19, 1819.

39. Ibid., March 30, 1816.

40. James B. Wiggins, Unidentified clipping, laid into the American Antiquarian Society copy of the *Catalogue of the Shakspeare Circulating Library . . .*, 1820.

41. J.O.C., Unidentified clipping, ibid.

42. Obit., *Missouri Republican*, July 23, 1833.

43. Alice J. G. Perkins and Theresa Wolfson, *Frances Wright: Free Enquirer* (N.Y.: Harper, 1939), pp. 195-97.

44. *Domestic Manners . . .*, p. 29.

45. New Orleans *Directory*, 1830.

46. James Stuart, *Three Years in North America*, 2 vols. (Edinburgh: Robert Cadell, 1833), 2: 212.

Chapter Five
Midcentury Onwards, A Single Dimension

Circulating libraries, which had from their beginnings contained a larger percentage of novels than had other contemporary institutions, found their collections after midcentury becoming even more predominantly fiction than they had been before. This shift did not result from major changes in the public reading preference, however, since fiction was as much sought in the first half of the century as it was in the second. Rather the increasing availability of nonfiction books free through the growing numbers of public and philanthropic libraries tended to draw off whatever residue of nonfiction use the circulating libraries had to that time sustained. Public and philanthropic libraries, on the other hand, when indeed they handled fiction at all, almost uniformly understocked it so that the circulating libraries came increasingly to be viewed, both by the public and by their proprietors, as purveyors solely of fiction, and in many cases as the most effective purveyors of fiction. This single dimension was their hallmark through the end of the nineteenth and into the twentieth centuries.

Rise of Free Libraries

Tax-Supported Libraries. Although public monies had in a few isolated cases been used to support free libraries earlier, the first extensive program of tax-based libraries came in 1835 with the passage in New York State of legislation paving the way for the establishment there of school district libraries. These were not, it should be noted, school libraries but were rather libraries administered by the school districts for the use of the general public, adults as well as children. The widespread felt need for free libraries elsewhere is demonstrated by the alacrity with which other states followed New York's lead in this matter. In 1837 Michigan and Massachusetts adopted somewhat similar legislation, as did Connecticut in 1839, Iowa and Rhode Island in 1840, and Indiana in 1841. By 1876 fully nineteen of the then thirty-six states had provided legislation making free or subsidized public library service available through the school districts.[1]

For a multiplicity of reasons which are interesting although too complex to go into here, the school district library movement failed. One primary cause for the failure, however, does affect this study. That was the lack of book selection expertise in the local communities; schoolmasters and board members simply did not have the scholarly and bibliographical acumen necessary to make the library collections meaningful educational and cultural forces in the districts. Various methods were tried to repair this critical deficiency at the local level. Some publishing houses issued standard sets of carefully preselected titles—"instant libraries" that could be bought en bloc by the districts. In other cases state departments of education prepared lists of approved or recommended titles. These devices often resulted in the availability of rather well-balanced regimens of reading in the district collections, although great care was exercised to assure that no books were acquired that represented unpopular political persuasions, religious heterodoxy, or views that could threaten the established morality of the communities.

Conservatism from within and strictures from without effectively debarred fiction from the shelves of these early tax-supported libraries. Public school officials Henry S. Randall of New York State and Horace Mann

(87)

of Massachusetts[2] both animadverted darkly upon the social ills that could result from the accessibility in school district libraries, especially to young people, of novels portraying "improper" morality. Although Mann did allow that "reading, merely for amusement, has its fit occasions," the school district libraries for the most part forewent acquiring any but the safest fiction in order to keep as far away from controversy as possible. If people in the school districts wanted novels, they could get them at their friendly circulating libraries, and they did.

Public libraries, in the current sense of that term, began appearing at midcentury to supersede the faltering school district library systems. Although these public libraries were uncomfortable, and remained so well into the present century, about supplying fiction across their counters, they never so completely eschewed it as did their school district precursors. There were several reasons for this. In the first place, public libraries as first conceived tended to be essentially adult institutions, and adults were presumably less to be misguided by "low," "trashy," "improper" fiction than the children who were numbered among the patrons of the school district libraries. Also, the public libraries came more directly out of the social library tradition, where some fiction had usually been allowed, albeit never apparently in quantities commensurate with the demand for it. Fiction had comprised between five and twenty-four percent of the holdings of the twelve New England social libraries between 1785 and 1841 analyzed by Shera,[3] but what scanty evidence exists about actual use of books in the social libraries suggests that fiction circulated in disproportionately higher numbers.[4]

George Ticknor expressed a very liberal sentiment, which would have been unwelcome to many Americans, when he proposed in 1851 that the Boston Public Library then abuilding should furnish any popular books . . . , in such numbers of copies that many persons, if they desired it, could be reading the same book at the same time; in short, that not only the best books of all sorts, but the pleasant literature of the day, should be made accessible to the whole people at the only time when they care for it, i.e. when it is fresh and new.[5]

Even Ticknor's acquaintance and sometime correspondent, Thomas Jefferson, although ever a supporter of libraries for the public,[6] held a strongly contrasting view of the social utility of fiction. He had cautioned in 1818 that

A great obstacle to good education is the inordinate passion prevalent for novels, and the time lost in that reading which should be instructively employed. When this poison infects the mind, it destroys its tone, and revolts it against wholesome reading. Reason and fact, plain and unadorned, are rejected. Nothing can engage attention unless dressed in all the figments of fancy; and nothing so bedecked comes amiss. The result is a bloated imagination, sickly judgment, and disgust towards all the real business of life.

Jefferson mitigated his harsh judgment only slightly; an occasional novel, he allowed, might manifest redeeming quality.

This mass of trash, however, [he continued] is not without some distinction; some few modelling their narratives, altho fictitious, on the incidents of real life, have been able to make them interesting and useful vehicles of a sound morality.[7]

If Jefferson was troubled about the popularity of fiction in 1818, he would have been appalled three decades later. Whereas only 28 American novels had been published between 1810 and 1819, fully 765 were published between 1840 and 1849. The number continued rising through the balance of the century: 2,933 appeared between midcentury and 1875, and 6,175 between then and 1900.[8] The public appetite for novels seemed never to abate.

Jefferson's apprehensions about fiction and similar views held by many other Americans to the contrary notwithstanding, Ticknor's proposal for stocking novels in the Boston Public Library did prevail,[9] bringing with it an unease for public librarians that was to last at least a century. Subsequent decades witnessed a continuing public discussion of whether or not public libraries should provide novels, and if so, in what quantities. It is testimony to the pragmatism of the American library community that almost no public librarians argued either that libraries should stock no fiction at all or that they should stock as much as the public would read; the great issue among librarians rather concerned the search for a tenable middle ground, a search that proved to be as tantalizing and almost as frustrating as the search for the Holy Grail.

The story of this bibliothecal odyssey has been well told elsewhere[10] and will not be repeated here. In general, however, the key arguments raised by those at the conservative end of the spectrum included the following:

1) Fiction deals with unreality rather than with truths.

2) It leads to impiety and the moral disintegration of society.

3) Novel reading diminishes the time available for more utilitarian pursuits.

4) Novels are an opiate that dulls the intellect.

5) Fiction breeds discontent with one's lot in life.

6) Most fiction is bad art.

7) Public funds should not be used to frivolous ends.

8) Librarians as civil servants must protect society.

Primary arguments at the liberal end of the scale included the following, some of which interestingly represent the obverse of those above:

1) Reading tastes improve as more reading takes place.
2) Novels awaken the imagination.
3) Novel-reading keeps people from more vicious pursuits.
4) The library belongs to the public, and the public wants novels.
5) Fiction can bring relief from the tedium of real-world hardships.
6) Some novels are high art.
7) Novels can insinuate morality.
8) Anything read has some value.
9) Librarians must be careful not to censor.

The results of this feckless ambivalence could probably be guessed; public libraries uniformly supplied some fiction, but just as uniformly not as much as the public wanted. Studies in the latter decades of the nineteenth century regularly reported that from 60 to 80 percent of the circulation in public libraries of the land comprised fiction,[11] although practically no one allowed that similar percentages of the collections should be novels. The leading library textbook at the end of the century proposed that fiction might well constitute about one-fifth of a public library's holdings, and the compilers of the first *ALA Catalog* in 1893 conceptualized "as nearly as possible the 5000 books that a new library ought to obtain first for its collection," of which less than fifteen percent was fiction.[12]

There was no such reluctance on the part of public

librarians to constrain the use of nonfiction by their patrons. Patron desires for books other than novels were met to the utmost limitations of the budget. This untrammeled availability of nonfiction in the free public libraries siphoned away all demand for such books from the circulating libraries of the time, while the parsimonious doling out of occasional "best" novels by the public libraries had just the opposite impact on novel-readers. As a result the circulating libraries, commercial agencies always able to trim services promptly in accord with public whim, foreshortened their collections of nonfiction and increased the representation of novels on their shelves to the point where the latter was virtually all that they had on hand.

Philanthropic Libraries. The entire responsibility for this change, however, cannot be ascribed to the new public libraries. The growing numbers of other kinds of libraries, mostly philanthropic, following 1850 had a similar impact and tended to hasten the process. These philanthropic libraries included those sponsored by the Sunday Schools, the YMCAs, and other welfare agencies.

The Sunday School libraries,[13] which began to come into prominence in the later 1820s, were intended to provide reading material for the young pupils in the Sunday Schools, which were at that time considered to be alternative educational enterprises. In the early years of the movement, these collections comprised primarily books of doctrine and biblical exegesis, tracts and sermons, and other exhortations to morality. By the 1840s, however, even the Sunday School library collections had come to have a strong fictional cast to them, although the stories they contained were based upon highly didactic themes and were strongly pietistic in tone. One collection dating from 1845 was fully one-fourth fiction.

More than half of these books contained, as a part of the title or in the preface, a statement that the tale was true. Most of them concerned young persons but not children; 90 per cent contained at least one death-bed scene. In all of the stories emphasis was upon the goodness exemplified. . . .[14]

In the words of one historian of Sunday School libraries, their holdings by 1860 "did not differ greatly from those to be found in the typical public library of the time."[15]

It has been estimated that there were some 30,000[16] Sunday School libraries in the United States in 1859, most if not all of which were supplying didactic fiction to young people. Depending upon one's view, they were either pandering to the lowest common denominator in their taste, or using these tales as carriers for messages of moral uplift. Certainly, however, they did in catering to young peoples' desire for fiction, whet their appetite for more, an appetite that was destined in their adult lives to be only partially slaked by the limited fiction holdings of the public libraries. In a sense, the Sunday School libraries could be viewed as generators of future customers for the brimming fiction collections of the circulating libraries of the latter half of the nineteenth century.

If the Sunday School libraries contributed to the increased use of fiction in the circulating libraries, the YMCA libraries had the opposite effect. It was the avowed intent of their founders

> to provide a suitable place for young men and others to spend their evenings in, without resorting to the haunts of vice and dissipation.[17]

Their frank adoption of this purpose meant that the YMCA collections had to contain much that was popular, including fiction. Since large segments of their book-stocks were gifts, however,—it is estimated that only about a quarter of their books were purchased[18]—the

YMCA libraries experienced some difficulty in keeping their collections attractive, but they appear to have succeeded nonetheless. The first YMCA was established in 1851, and only eight years later thirty were already operating libraries. Few were free, but most charged only a nominal fee; the amount most frequently paid by users was One Dollar per year.

Not only did YMCAs maintain libraries, but so also did other kinds of philanthropic agencies. Workingmen's institutes, boys' lodging houses, children's aid societies, city missions, churches, temperance organizations, and other benevolent groups and individual philanthropists sponsored libraries and reading rooms before, but especially after, midcentury. A primary effect of these efforts upon the circulating libraries was not that they reshaped their book collections but rather that they eliminated altogether the role that many had assumed earlier of providing subscription reading rooms to their communities. Following the Civil War there was virtually no market left for reading rooms operated for profit; they had been superseded by tax-based and philanthropic operations which could provide the service free. The discontinuation of this aspect of the work of some commercial libraries tended even more so than before to leave them with a single purpose—to circulate novels.

Responses from Circulating Libraries

The circulating libraries never questioned their role as the chief providers of fiction. The agony that pervaded the public library community over the morality and social utility of fiction appears never to have reached the commercial libraries. They remained throughout true to their basic purpose of turning a profit for their proprietors by supplying the books that their customers wanted when they wanted them. Occasional criticism of them appeared in editorials or was heard from the pulpits, but with the benefit of a little judicious self-policing the circulating libraries managed to conduct their business with impunity.

It is difficult to find many generalizations that can be postulated with certitude about circulating libraries during this era. Sources of information about them become much more diffuse than they were in the earlier period, and perhaps they are also less reliable. Some libraries obviously were quite large or had special characteristics that made them of noteworthy significance even in their own time. By far the majority of them, however, were quite small, and their modest impact was at best local.

A. K. Loring. Clearly one of the circulating libraries of consequence following midcentury was the Select Library of Aaron Kimball Loring, which he opened at 319 Washington Street, opposite Doane's Oyster House, in Boston in June of 1859.[19] Loring was only thirty-three years old at the time, but he had already learned his trade well as a clerk for many years in the bookselling firm of Phillips Sampson and Company. He had also come to know personally some of the leading members of Boston's outstanding literati—George Ticknor, Charles Devens, Wendell Phillips, Edward Everett, and others—whom he would later number among the patrons of his library. Perhaps more important still, Loring had learned, in the words of one contemporary, "the weaknesses of the great,—those who loved to hear their official titles emphasized before other customers, and also their tastes and whims."[20]

It was Loring's aim to make his institution Boston's equivalent of Mudie's Select Library in London, which had added almost a million volumes to its collections during the previous decade, doubtless the largest circulating library ever brought together![21] Loring started out on a much more modest scale. His first catalogue issued in 1860 contained only some 770 titles, of which five-sixths were fiction. His holdings grew apace, however, and fifteen years later he reported owning 10,000 volumes, hardly in a class with Mudie's, but one of the largest circulating libraries in the United States nonetheless.[22]

Also in emulation of Mudie's, which daily kept eight book vans on the streets of London delivering books to patrons, Loring for a time maintained a door-to-door service in Boston. This service, rendered first by boys and later by horsemen, reportedly "succeeded best in the less fashionable places like East Boston and Chelsea."[23] Loring did not take subscriptions to his library, preferring rather to rent his wares at the flat rate of Two Cents a day.

Although Loring continued his library into the 1880s, he increasingly conducted it in conjunction with other enterprises. He sold books (new books as well as surplus volumes withdrawn from his library), periodicals, and stationery. He soon established himself as a publisher of juvenile books, of which those by Horatio Alger, Jr. and Louisa May Alcott brought him by far the largest fame and fortune. He later removed his library to Bromfield Street and opened a cheap lunch counter in the basement where he served the temperance potables of the day, including "old-fashioned country Dier-Drink, compounded by Dr. Swett, from roots and herbs" for Five Cents a cup.[24] Ever an eccentric, however, Loring went bankrupt in 1881 and thereafter for a long time inhabited only the fringes of the Boston book world. He was described in 1903 as "still a kindly, bright old gentleman."[25] He lived on for eight years thereafter in the care of Boston's Home for Aged Men, dying in 1911.

William Brotherhead. Perhaps the largest circulating

library ever assembled in the United States belonged to William Brotherhead, a secondhand bookseller of Philadelphia. In 1860 Brotherhead winnowed a large selection of volumes from his sales collection and opened a library at 218 South Eighth Street. He was soon able to report that "the success of my library caused me to pay more attention to it than old-book selling, and this business of the library was my chief care."[26] In 1863 he removed his operation to 911 Locust Street, and then four years later he moved it again, this time to its permanent location on the first floor of a new home he had constructed at 205 South Thirteenth Street, where he also continued his bookselling in the basement.

Brotherhead maintained a very large selection of books, reported as 50,000 volumes in 1867, and 35,000 volumes in 1876.[27] His collection represented the finest popular literature published both in England and America, and his library became a fashionable resort for the elite of Philadelphia and environs. Brotherhead also borrowed a practice from Mudie's in London when he opened branches in several other cities, including Pottsville and Wilkes-Barre in Pennsylvania, Washington, D.C., Elkton, Maryland, and Dover, Delaware. In 1878 Brotherhead fell on the ice and injured his spine and was forced thereafter to relinquish his library and bookselling businesses.

James Hammond. The largest circulating library in New England before and after midcentury was that operated in Newport, Rhode Island, by James Hammond. Hammond had purchased the library in 1811 from Wanton & Rathbone, who had in turn acquired it from William R. Wilder in 1806. Wilder had established the library in Newport in 1798,[28] so the institution was one of venerable antiquity in the prosperous coastal community. Hammond, who also maintained a dry goods emporium, built the library carefully and well, and by

1852 he was able to offer 8,000 volumes to his patrons. Some 5,000 of the volumes were novels. The collection continued to grow, so that by 1857 it contained 9,000 volumes and by 1858 it contained 10,000. At his death Hammond bequeathed his library to his assistant who managed it for a time before discontinuing the business and auctioning off the collections for $2,500.[29] The library had served Newport readers for more than three score years.

Other Libraries. There were a handful of other libraries in the nation that maintained large holdings. In 1876 the American Eclectic Library in New York reported owning 30,300 volumes and the Book Exchange in Washington, D.C. claimed to have 10,000. The Librairie de la Famille, a multilingual library in New Orleans, in that year reported circulating its 25,000 volumes 50,000 times, but it was probably envious of the much higher circulation posted by its competitor in the Louisiana town, Ellis Circulating Library. Ellis claimed that its 9,000 volumes had circulated fully 150,000 times in 1875! Hawkins' Circulating Library in Brooklyn held some 17,000 volumes at the time, all in English or German fiction.[30]

By far the majority, however, of the ninety circulating libraries that reported their sizes to the U.S. Bureau of Education in 1876 were very much smaller than the few mentioned above. Although collections ranged from 300 to 35,000 volumes, the median size was only 1,000; in other words, half of the libraries reporting could number their volumes (not titles) in only three figures. Only thirty-three institutions reported both their sizes and their gross incomes to that 1876 survey, thereby permitting the calculation of earnings-per-volume. It is dangerous to make inferences from such a small number of instances, but the few examples reported ranged from 8 Cents to 85 Cents per volume per year, with the mean

(A 1 2 0) 1

JAMES HAMMOND'S
Circulating library,
No. 106, THAMES-STREET,
NEWPORT, R. I.

This Library contains more than
4,000 VOLUMES.
The **N E W W O R K S** are
Added as soon as published.

JAMES HAMMOND,
Has for sale at his Circulating Library,
DRY-GOODS, AND BOOK-STORE,
Letter paper—writing paper—quills—ink—pen-knifes—
pencils—wax—lines—visiting cards—playing cards,
dice—backgammon-bds.—chess-men,
dominos—and
S T A T I O N A R Y.

School—Juvenile—and Miscellaneous **BOOKS.**

Newman's, Reeves & Osborne's boxes of water colors and
PAINTING MATERIALS.

Color'd & gold paper, & materials for FANCY WORK.

Superior scented soap, Paris cologne, & Laven-
der; tooth-brushes, he d-brushes, & combs.

Trade Card of James Hammond's Circulating Library in Newport in the 1840s (Orig. 4½ x 3¼ inches). *Courtesy of the Amer-*
ican Antiquarian Society

(99)

at 40 Cents. Too few libraries indicated both number of circulations and earnings to permit any analysis at all to be made of those ratios. Apparently, however, it was not unreasonable for circulating library proprietors to hope for as many as ten circulations per volume per year; some got more than fifteen.

There is little that can be adduced about the number of readers who patronized the circulating libraries. The 1876 survey of libraries in the United States did not inquire as to numbers of patrons, although the less comprehensive survey of the 1850s did ask for such information. Thus we can know that in 1857 Winsor's Circulating Library in Providence lent to 2,000 borrowers, while Perrin's Circulating Library in the same city, lent to 2,500 persons in 1855.[31] Scanty evidence suggests, however, that a very small number of readers usually accounted for a large portion of the borrowings. The following anecdote, allegedly taking place just prior to midcentury, bespeaks the extent of novel reading by some individuals.

> Being with two gentlemen at a book store in New York, at which was kept a circulating library, one of them remarked that an acquaintance of his was accustomed to read two hundred volumes of novels a year. The other thought it incredible. The first, turning to the bookseller, asked what was the largest number of volumes drawn by one person from his library, in a year. Referring to his books, he found that a certain lady had taken four hundred and fifty sets, mostly two-volumed, making about nine hundred volumes.[32]

Such heavy readers doubtless availed themselves of the annual subscription rates, usually ranging in the 1860s and 1870s from $3.50 to $6, rather than the per-book charge of about Two Cents per day.

It is difficult to see how library proprietors could get an adequate return on their investment at these rates. Certainly few got rich. Except for a handful of the better known establishments, little information can be gleaned as to how long they remained in business after their initial openings. The 1876 survey of *Public Libraries* reported data, however, that suggest that most circulating libraries may have been short-lived. Table 3 shows that more than three-fourths of the eighty libraries reporting their founding dates to that survey had been in existence for less than a decade. The Civil War clearly had had its debilitating effect, as no new libraries were reported as having been established in 1863 and only one in 1864.

TABLE 3

Longevity of Libraries Reporting to 1876 Survey

Age	Number
1-5 years	34
6-10 years	27
11-15 years	8
16-20 years	3
21-25 years	3
More than 25 years	5
Total	80

Even this, however, does not speak to the matter of the "mortality rate" of circulating libraries. Perhaps the best one can do in this regard is deduce from negative evidence. Table 4 shows that forty-eight circulating libraries identified in the course of the present study as having operated after 1850 were not listed in the 1876 volume on *Public Libraries*, the implication being that they were no longer in business. It must be recognized here that this is a very shaky basis for argument, as a multiplicity of explanations other than their demise might account for the absence of these institutions from the 1876 volume. Notwithstanding the lack of hard evidence, however, the impression persists that many, perhaps even most, of the circulating libraries during these years were of quite brief duration.

TABLE 4

Post-1850 Libraries Not Listed in 1876 Survey

Latest Date Known	Number
1851-1855	3
1856-1860	22
1861-1865	14
1866-1870	5
1871-1875	4
Total	48

As the number of circulating libraries grew with the nation's population, but as their average size and profitability and perhaps also their average longevity declined, fewer of them found it in their interest to publish catalogues of their holdings than had been the case in earlier decades. Only nine printed catalogues from the post-1850 era were located in the course of this study, although it is known that some others existed. The number of titles listed in these nine catalogues ranges from 365 to 4,320, with a mean figure of 920, close to the aforementioned mean figure of 1,000 volumes held by the institutions reporting to the 1876 survey. The holdings represented in these catalogues are heavily fiction, ranging from 55 to 97 percent, with a mean percentage of 81.

This 81 percent fiction in the circulating libraries must, to be understood, be compared with the fiction component in other libraries of the period. As was mentioned earlier, public librarians toward the end of the century were suggesting that their collections ought to contain only about 20 percent fiction. In a survey conducted in 1893, it was found that respondent public libraries held fiction in a range from 10 to 45 percent of their collections, with an average figure of 24 percent.[33] An analysis of the catalogues of mercantile library holdings between midcentury and 1865 indicates that the fiction holdings of fourteen institutions ranged from 12.1 to 41.2 percent, with a median figure of 22.7.[34] In other words, it appears that the average circulating library following 1850 invested between three and four times as much of its resources in fiction as did its contemporary public and associational institutions.

Cheap Publishing and Hard Times

The single factor most responsible for the decline in the fortunes of the circulating libraries following the Civil War therefore was not competition from free public libraries. That changed them but did not kill them. They declined rather because of cheap publishing.[35] In the early years of the century most novels had been published in the United States in two volumes at prices ranging between $1.50 and $2. Expansion of markets in the 1820s and 1830s, however, permitted larger press runs, and such technological innovations as stereotyping introduced economies of production, so that book prices by 1835 were losing their stability. The process was hastened around 1840 when publishers began issuing paper-bound novels in parts and as supplements to periodicals so that they could be mailed at preferred rates, both practices depressing book prices far below what they had been previously, some soon going for as little as 12½ to 15 Cents apiece. A postal ruling in 1844, however, required that such publications thereafter be posted book-rate, thereby mitigating for a time the impact of cheap publishing on book availability. Novel prices stabilized for more than a decade at around 50 Cents in paper and 75 Cents in cloth.

Cheap publishing was to return, however. In 1860 the appearance of Beadle's Dime Novel, No.1 anticipated a flood of cheap books that inundated the land for more than three decades thereafter. Utilizing progressively improving technology, exceptionally cheaper paper following the introduction of woodpulp in 1867, and aggressive marketing practices; permitting production standards to decline; and benefitting from increasingly favorable postal rates (One Cent per pound after 1885), the absence until 1891 of protection of the rights of foreign authors under American law, and ever larger markets as the nation's population grew at unprecedented rates, publishers virtually glutted the reading market with novels that often retailed as low as a nickel apiece.

Such stiff competition drove many circulating libraries to the wall, especially those that had been marginal in the first place. Who would rent for Two Cents a day a book that could be bought for a nickel? Library proprietors responded in various ways to the challenge of cheap books. Some of those that survived did so by paring costs to the bone, others enlarged their operations so as to benefit from economies of scale, and a few succeeded by giving more highly personalized book service than could be obtained elsewhere in the community.

Some circulating library proprietors, finding their operations no longer profitable, donated or sold their collections to the newer local public libraries. Frederick Leypoldt, who had maintained a circulating library and reading room at the corner of Chestnut and Juniper Streets in Philadelphia, sold his 6,000-volume collection to the Mercantile Library in 1864.[36] Denison & Burdick's Circulating Library in Elgin, Illinois, sold its 700 volumes to the newly-established public library there in 1874.[37] In Muncie, Indiana, in 1868 Postmaster H. C.

Marsh accepted the books from the defunct county library and merged them into his circulating library with the understanding that he would lend them free; seven years later he turned them over, and sold his own books to the new Muncie Public Library where they became the nucleus for its collections.[38] At the end of the century the Charleston, Illinois, Circulating Library gave 114 volumes to the new public library then commencing in that place.[39]

In other cases, circulating library collections suffered less propitious fates. William Brotherhead, once finding himself overstocked, was able to get more for his surplus books as pulp at the paper mill than he could get for them at auction, even though, in his words, it was "a very fine collection of old folios and quartos, and many good books."[40] Some circulating library collections were lost in fires. Cobb's Library in Chicago lost 5,000 volumes in the Great Fire of 1871, a contemporary newspaper account explaining that the "Library House was demolished with gunpowder in the vain hope of saving the large building near by."[41] Woodruff's Circulating Library in Little Rock suffered losses in 1863 which could be indirectly attributed to fire; books from the library were apparently removed into the street one night out of apprehension of a fire in an adjacent building, and many of them were carried off by Union troops then billeted in the town.[42]

In many circulating libraries the traditional practice of soliciting annual subscriptions gave way to the less cumbersome process of charging daily rentals. In fact, these institutions came increasingly to be called "rental libraries" as the nineteenth century closed and the twentieth century began. Many also began utilizing more advanced marketing methods, especially enlarging their financial bases by opening branches. It was mentioned earlier that William Brotherhead had maintained several branches in the 1860s. Others did likewise. The West Side Library in Chicago operated branches throughout that city in the 1870s and 1880s,[43] as did Wilson's Circulating Library in Pennsylvania and New Jersey at about the same time.[44]

The maintenance of branches often gave way to the establishment of chains. The American Circulating Libraries were operated in the 1880s by Allen & Company, booksellers of Hillsdale, Michigan; if a community could sign up enough subscribers at One Dollar per year, Allen would place there a prepackaged library of some 400 titles and keep it active.[45] The H. Parmelee Library Company, which was initiated in Des Moines in 1882 but soon moved to 1841 Wabash Avenue in Chicago, had a somewhat similar plan. By subscribing to a particular amount a town or neighborhood was entitled to the use of 2,000 volumes for two years, sent by Parmelee in installments of fifty books. Parmelee also encouraged the establishment of book clubs and would, for a fee, arrange for home delivery.[46] The Booklovers' Library was founded in Philadelphia in 1900; it offered services nationwide and would for a service charge deliver books to homes or deposit circulating collections in factories, shops, and even Sunday Schools.[47] Such extensive operations as these enabled the libraries to purchase large numbers of copies of a book on a single invoice, thereby qualifying for publishers' maximum discounts.

American rental libraries appear never to have become as influential as Mudie's of London, however, which as a standard practice often arranged to buy up the whole printing of a promising novel.[48] It was an anomaly in the minds of some that in the United States, world-renowned for its commercial acumen and its commitment to the profit motive, the circulating library never rose to the same heights that it did in England.

Even the *Christian Science Monitor* found the matter somewhat puzzling.

> For some reason or another [it opined in 1919] the circulating library has not taken root in America. . . . Useful and agreeable as the American system of [public] lending libraries is, it hardly takes the place of the English circulating library. The public libraries of America, with the best intentions, are seldom able to supply the newest books. A determined Englishman can make Mudie supply him with the newest books. Besides, calling for a book and having it left at your house are very different things. To many people in England a compensation for living in a remote part of the country is the arrival of the weekly Mudie box.[49]

The cause of this apparent aberration in the American mercantile instinct seems to lie in the public library community's continuing equivocation regarding fiction. If it never quite opted for it, neither did it opt against it. By supplying some fiction, the public library never quite permitted the circulating libraries in the United States to become strong. For a long time there was a kind of unarticulated territorial agreement between the public and circulating libraries. Melvil Dewey had implied it as early as 1888, when he observed:

> Surely every library ought to have an ambition to get and preserve books, and surely some place should be found in every general collection for fiction and humor. These ought, however, to be the embroidery, and not the web. A circulating library, run as a business, will of course take on the latter character.[50]

After several decades of respecting one another's territorial prerogatives, the circulating and public libraries came in the 1910s into conflict. The conflict arose when public libraries began laying in special collections of duplicate copies of the most popular books of the day to be rented to patrons rather than circulated free. This in effect placed tax-supported libraries into direct business competition with private enterprise and created considerable animosity between the two kinds of establishments where essentially amicable relations had prevailed previously. A key complaint from the circulating libraries, which were then having to charge a rather standard Three Cents daily for popular books, was that public libraries, with space and staff paid for from tax monies, were undercutting them with charges of Two Cents per day for the same books. Some circulating libraries even litigated for injunctive relief from such "unfair competition," but the new practice was never completely put to rest.[51] In fact, it eventually became a very widespread procedure among public libraries to circulate recent popular books from duplicate collections and to charge readers a fee for the privilege.

This step by public libraries had a further debilitating effect upon the traditional circulating libraries operating out of bookstores, but it still did not kill them. Some independent libraries flourished nonetheless,[52] but the development did force the rental chains and news services even more so than they had earlier to decentralize their activities. In the later 1920s and 1930s, as many now recall, the rental bookracks became standard paraphernalia in drug and department stores, soda fountains, railroad and bus stations, and in other convenient locations. Some chains, especially in the larger cities, operated weekly delivery services throughout office buildings, while others increased their home deliveries either by mail or messenger, an activity seldom engaged in by the public libraries. The result was more rental outlets but smaller collections. In 1932 Frederic Melcher, editor of *Publishers' Weekly,* estimated that there were then some 35,000 rental libraries in the nation with collections ranging in size from 50 to 10,000 volumes but averaging only 150 books per library.[53] This was only one-tenth to one-twentieth the size of the average American circulating library a century earlier. How much they had changed!

Decline of the Circulating Library

Of all the vicissitudes, changes, and challenges that circulating libraries ever had to face in their two hundred year existence in the United States, the advent of television was the most deleterious. As late as 1948 *Publishers' Weekly* could report that "the rental library business still was good," but only six years later a survey of circulating library proprietors revealed that much had happened to alter that assessment. Of those responding to the survey, made in March of 1954, 20 percent reported that they had discontinued their libraries in the previous twenty-four months, 12 percent indicated that they planned to close their libraries soon, and another 38 percent said that their libraries were no longer profitable. Fewer than one-third foresaw business continuing as usual. Table 5 itemizes the principal reasons given for the decline in their fortunes.[54]

TABLE 5

Reasons Cited for Decline in Rentals

Television	41
Paperback publishing	30
High cost of books	15
Public library competition	9
Book clubs, premiums, etc.	8
Poor quality of books	8
Poor chain service	8
Magazine serializations	4

Circulating libraries had for more than a century been contending with all of these problems, save for the leading one—television.

Never more than marginally profitable in America, except in a notable minority, most rental library ventures in the nation disappeared in the 1950s. The once ubiquitous rental bookracks slowly faded from the scene, and the rental departments in most bookstores were quietly closed down. A few traditional circulating libraries survive even to the present time, but they are today viewed almost as novelties, where once they were a common part of a community's cultural accoutrements.

Yet even now the commercial library is not dead in the United States, although its principal manifestation today is much transmogrified from what it once was. Today's vestige of the once-prominent circulating library melds the profit motivation of that original institution with the egalitarian mystique of the public library movement. In the late 1940s commercial interests commenced offering to provide the rental books needed in the public libraries. The offers were widely accepted, and the so-called "McNaughton Plan" soon came into extensive use. Originally the rental charges for books borrowed from public libraries under this plan were paid by the readers themselves, exactly as they had done when the public libraries were running their own rental collections, and exactly as they had done when they borrowed from circulating libraries. Later, however, most public libraries began to find it expedient to pay the rental charges out of public funds rather than passing the cost on to the reader. Thus today taxpayers are paying the charges for books rented from commercial libraries passed through the middle-man, which is the public library. Who a century or two ago could have foreseen such an eventuality?

Summary

Circulating library collections following midcentury comprised almost solely fiction, as the new free libraries took away their previous customers for nonfiction while refusing to do the same for novel-readers. The rise of free reading rooms drove those supported by subscription out of business. Cheap publishing in the 1870s and after forced new business methods upon those circulating libraries that survived. Primary among these new methods was the development of chains of small rental bookracks in such locations as drugstores and railroad stations. In the early twentieth century public libraries installed rental collections of their own, but in the 1940s they began contracting these rental operations to commercial suppliers, as under the McNaughton Plan, thereby effecting an alliance between the public and commercial libraries. In the 1950s television almost, but not quite, killed the remaining market for rental books.

REFERENCES

1. Carleton B. Joeckel, *The Government of the American Public Library* (Chicago: University of Chicago Libraries, 1935), pp. 8-13; Henry L. Cecil and Willard A. Heaps, *School Library Service in the United States* (N.Y.: H. W. Wilson, 1940), pp. 41-47.

2. Sidney Ditzion, "The District-School Library, 1835-55," *Library Quarterly* 10 (October 1940): 545-77.

3. Jesse Shera, *Foundations of the Public Library* (Chicago: University of Chicago Press, 1949), p. 103.

4. Frank Monaghan and Marvin Lowenthal, *This Was New York, the Nation's Capital in 1789* (N.Y.: Doubleday Doran, 1943), p. 151, indicates that 35 percent of the books charged out of the New York Society Library in 1789-90 were fiction, although novels constituted only 17 percent of the collection. Almost exactly the same ratios (*e.g.*, one-third and one-eighth

respectively) prevailed in the Union Library Company of Brunswick, N.J., in 1796; see *Library Journal* 14 (July 1889): 322.

5. George Ticknor, *Life, Letters, and Journals*, 2 vols. (Boston: James R. Osgood & Co., 1876), 2: 301-02.

6. In 1809 Jefferson had written to John Wyche "I have often thought that nothing would do more extensive good at small expense than the establishment of a small circulating library in every county, to consist of a few well-chosen books, to be lent to the people of the country." Thomas Jefferson, *Writings*, 20 vols. (Washington, D.C.: Thomas Jefferson Memorial Association, 1907), 11: 282.

7. Ibid., 15: 166.

8. Lyle H. Wright, "Statistical Survey of American Fiction, 1774-1850," *Huntington Library Quarterly* 2 (April 1939): 309; *American Fiction, 1851-1875* (San Marino, Cal.: Huntington Library, 1965); *American Fiction, 1876-1900* (San Marino, Cal.: Huntington Library, 1966).

9. The BPL's liberal fiction policy became a source of bitter controversy in the 1880s, however. See Esther Jane Carrier, *Fiction in Public Libraries, 1876-1900* (New York: Scarecrow, 1965), pp. 234-55.

10. Ibid., passim.

11. Edwin H. Woodruff, "Fiction in Public Libraries," *Library Journal* 20 (October 1895): 343; John Cotton Dana, "Fiction in Libraries," *Current Literature* 33 (August 1902): 233. Note also the following anonymous parody entitled "Fiction Song," *Library Journal* 15 (November 1890): 325:

FICTION SONG

At a library desk stood some readers one day
   Crying "Novels, oh, novels, oh, novels!"
And I said to them, "People, oh, why do you say
   "Give us novels, oh, novels, oh, novels?"
Is it weakness of intellect, people, I cried,
Or simply a space where the brains should abide?"
They answered me not, or they only replied,
   "Give us novels, oh, novels, oh, novels!"

Here are thousands of books that will do you more good
   Than the novels, oh, novels, oh, novels!
You will weaken your brain with such poor mental food
   As the novels, oh, novels, oh, novels!

Pray take history, music, or travels, or plays,
Biography, poetry, science, essays
Or anything else that more wisdom displays
    Than the novels, oh, novels, oh, novels!

A librarian may talk till he's black in the face
    About novels, oh, novels, oh, novels!
And may think that with patience he may raise the taste
    Above novels, oh, novels, oh, novels!
He may talk till with age his round shoulders are bent
And the white hairs of time 'mid the black ones are sent,
When he hands his report in still seventy per cent
    Will be novels, oh, novels, oh, novels!

12. John Cotton Dana, *A Library Primer* (Chicago: Library Bureau, 1899), p. 43; U.S. Bureau of Education, *Catalog of "A.L.A. Library"* (Washington, D.C.: Government Printing Office, 1893), p. v.

13. F. Allen Briggs, "The Sunday School Library in the Nineteenth Century," *Library Quarterly* 31 (April 1961): 166-77; Frank K. Walter, "A Poor but Respectable Relation; The Sunday-School Library," *Library Quarterly* 12 (July 1942): 731-39.

14. Briggs, ibid., 174.

15. Ibid., 173.

16. William J. Rhees, *Manual of Public Libraries, Institutions, and Societies, in the United States* (Philadelphia: J. B. Lippincott, 1859), p. xxviii.

17. Ibid., p. 523.

18. Doris M. Fletcher, "Read a Book and Sin No More: The Early YMCA Libraries," *Wilson Library Bulletin* 31 (March 1957): 521-22.

19. Madeleine B. Stern, *Imprints on History* (Bloomington: Indiana University Press, 1956), pp. 179-80.

20. Charles K. Bolton, "Circulating Libraries in Boston, 1765-1865," *Publications of the Colonial Society of Massachusetts* 11 (February 1907): 207.

21. By the end of the century Mudie's had acquired an estimated seven and a half million books. See Guinevere L. Griest, *Mudie's Circulating Library and the Victorian Novel* (Bloomington: Indiana University Press, 1970), p. 21.

22. U.S. Bureau of Education, *Public Libraries in the United States of America . . . . Special Report. Part 1.* (Washington, D.C.: Government Printing Office, 1876), p. 1052.

23. Bolton, "Circulating Libraries . . . ," 207.
24. "Dull Times," *Publishers' Weekly* 12 (July 7, 1877): 6; *Town Topics* 18 (September 15, 1887): 7.
25. Bolton, "Circulating Libraries . . . ," 207.
26. William Brotherhead, *Forty Years among the Old Booksellers of Philadelphia* (Philadelphia: A. P. Brotherhead, 1891), p. 17.
27. Ibid., p. 18; U.S. Bureau of Education, *Public Libraries* . . . , p. 1120.
28. H. Glenn Brown and Maude O. Brown, *A Directory of Printing, Publishing, Bookselling & Allied Trades in Rhode Island to 1865* (N.Y.: New York Public Library, 1958), pp. 80-81, 183.
29. Shera, *Foundations* . . . , p. 146.
30. U.S. Bureau of Education, *Public Libraries* . . . , pp. 768, 1022, 1044, 1043, 1084.
31. Rhees, *Manual of Public Libraries*, pp. 447, 440.
32. [John Mitchell], *Reminiscences of Scenes and Characters in College* (New Haven, Conn.: A. H. Maltby, 1847), pp. 57-58.
33. U.S. Bureau of Education, *Report of the Commissioner of Education, 1892-93* (Washington, D.C.: Government Printing Office, 1895), pp. 935-36.
34. William D. Boyd, Jr., "Books for Young Businessmen: Mercantile Libraries in the United States" (Ph.D. dissertation, Indiana University, 1975), pp. 162, 167.
35. Most of the material in the next two paragraphs is drawn from John Tebbel, *History of Book Publishing in the United States*, 2 vols. (N.Y.: R. R. Bowker, 1972-75), 1: 243-50; 2: 481-88, 493-96.
36. Adolf Growoll, *Book Trade Bibliography in the United States in the Nineteenth Century* (N.Y.: Burt Franklin, 1939), pp. lxviii-lxx.
37. Katharine L. Sharp, *Illinois Libraries* (Urbana: University of Illinois, 1907), p. [175].
38. W. E. Henry, comp., *Municipal and Institutional Libraries of Indiana* (n.p.: Louisiana Purchase Exposition Commission of Indiana, 1904), pp. 104-05.
39. Sharp, *Illinois Libraries*, p. [163].
40. Brotherhead, *Forty Years* . . . , p. 33.
41. *Chicago Tribune*, October 26, 1871.
42. B. L. Hutchens, "Arkansas Enjoyed Libraries and Books Back in the 1840's," *Arkansas Libraries* 6 (October 1949): 11-12.

43. Gwladys Spencer, "The Chicago Public Library; Origins and Background" (Ph.D. dissertation, University of Chicago, 1940), p. 113.

44. J. Scharf and Thompson Westcott, *History of Philadelphia*, 3 vols. (Philadelphia: L. H. Everts, 1884), 3: 1228.

45. A catalogue advertising this Company's wares in 1886 is preserved in the Library of Congress.

46. Sharp, *Illinois Libraries*, p. [632].

47. Ibid., p. [500].

48. Griest, *Mudie's Circulating Library* . . . .

49. Quoted in "Are Subscription Circulating Libraries Needed?" *Library Journal* 44 (December 1919): 778.

50. Melvil Dewey, "Libraries As Related to the Educational Work of the State," *Report of the Commissioner of Education for the Year 1887-88* (Washington, D.C.: Government Printing Office, 1889), p. 1035.

51. "Rental Library vs. Public Library," *Publishers' Weekly* 104 (August 11, 1923): 486: "Rental Libraries Public and Private," ibid., 104 (August 18, 1923): 544-45; "Rental Library Competition," ibid., 541-42.

52. For a summary account of some of the larger independent circulating libraries in the 1930s, see "Present Rental Library Practice, Part II," ibid., 132 (September 25, 1937): 1318-22.

53. Frederic G. Melcher, "Should Popular Demand for Current Ephemeral Books Be Met by Rental Libraries? Yes!" *American Library Association Bulletin* 26 (September 1932): 708.

54. Groff Conklin, "Rental Libraries: Problems and Prospects—Part 1," *Publishers' Weekly* 165 (April 24, 1954): 1818-19.

Chapter Six
Their Role in American
Library Development

Thus there has not been a time in more than two centuries when American entrepreneurs were not purveying library services for gain somewhere. Many of their ventures have failed financially; others have been at best marginally profitable. Some, however, have clearly been successful business enterprises, returning adequate livelihood to their proprietors over sustained periods of time. It may be that their failure rate has been neither markedly higher nor lower than those in other private-sector industries.

How has it happened that commercial libraries have so long been viable commercial investments, especially in more recent times when they have seemingly had to compete with free, tax-based public libraries? How have they managed to survive the extensive changes that have taken place in the nation's political, social, and literary environments since 1762? What has been the source of their strength, the wellspring of their continuing vigor? These and related issues will be reviewed in the ensuing paragraphs.

Initiatives of the Circulating Libraries

In retrospect, it appears that much of the lasting power of the commercial library movement in this nation has resulted from its willingness to initiate. A surprising number of library innovations have come out of the circulating libraries. The profit incentive apparently has been a continuing stimulant goading circulating library proprietors to try new services when others would not, or when there appeared to be social ambivalence, or even resistance, to them. Many of these initiatives, once they proved their utility in the circulating libraries, became wrapped into the standard practices of other kinds of libraries as well.

Probably of greatest significance among these initiatives was the willingness of the circulating libraries from the start to serve women. Whereas very few other eighteenth-century American libraries would even allow women on their premises, the circulating libraries by contrast openly sought their patronage. William Rind's first advertisement in 1762 made clear that his books were available to "Gentlemen and Ladies." Wood and Gifford in Charleston made the same representations in 1763 and 1772 respectively. Loudon reported from New York in 1774 that "the ladies are his best customers," and following 1770 Nicola in Philadelphia operated his library in the same stand with a milliner.

Even in the early years of the nineteenth century when other kinds of libraries were beginning slowly to admit women, the circulating libraries continued to be most attentive to their reading needs. Many of the proprietors were themselves women; in fact, the first female librarians in this country were custodians of commercial libraries, an initiative of some consequence in its own right. Circulating libraries were increasingly maintained in locations frequented by women. In 1809 Hunter & Robinson of Baltimore advertised that their manuscript catalogue "could be examined in the Library Room, or sent out to the ladies, if required."[1] Some libraries would also arrange to have their books delivered to women in their homes, if considerations of decorum prevented them from coming to the shops. Circulating libraries sometimes provided separate entrances for women, while others maintained special reading rooms for them.

Akin to their initiative in serving women, the circulating libraries also pioneered in the circulation of popular books, striving always to supply the books people wanted to read in numbers commensurate with the public appetite. This meant that the representation of fiction and *belles-lettres* on their shelves always bulked larger than it did in the holdings of other contemporary institutions. From the beginning they considered it their responsibility to serve the public taste rather than to raise it. Librarians in other kinds of institutions have tended through the decades to follow this initiative of the commercial libraries, albeit usually with reluctance and often at a distance.

These two initiatives—to cater to women and to supply what the public wanted to read—brought down considerable calumny upon the circulating libraries. "Slopshops in literature," they were called, "evergreen trees of diabolical knowledge,"[2] because of their unabashed trafficking in "low" or "unfit" novels to "young" and "impressionable" females.

> How my heart aches when I see lovely girls just emerged from childhood [wrote one editor in 1803], nay sometimes not more than ten or twelve years of age, allowed to have free access to the circulating libraries, and suffered to read whatever book, chance or fashion may put into their hands.[3]

It was not only men who were concerned about the use of circulating libraries by women. Even novelist Susanna Rowson fretted about "the female head" which was "well stored with sensibility, and all the delicate feelings gleaned from a circulating library, the contents of which she has eagerly and indiscriminately perused."[4] For almost a century following the appearance in London in 1797 of an essay entitled "Novel Reading, A Cause of Female Depravity,"[5] the American press and pulpit told and retold horror stories about women who lost their reason as a result of reading too much fiction.[6]

Only a few circulating library proprietors argued in support of novel-reading, Caritat being the outstanding example. Most protested rather that they took great care to stock only such books as would not offend the moral standards of the community. John Dabney of Salem defined his selection policy as follows in 1791:

> A Circulating Library, like the volume of Nature, is found to be an interesting Miscellany, but composed of an assemblage of productions extremely opposite in their nature and tendency. Many of these productions are known to be highly beneficial, others very agreeable and engaging; and some it will be added, are injurious to Society. If as many of the latter are excluded as *possible,* and an arrangement be formed of the most eligible, it may be considered not only as a Repository of Rational Amusement, but as a Museum, from Whence may be derived materials capable of forming the minds of individuals to solid virtue, true politeness, the noblest actions, and the purest benevolence.[7]

Hunter & Robinson of Baltimore laid in a stock representing "all branches of literature, but not eschewing the novel, although selecting them carefully."[8] Samuel Angell of Warren, Rhode Island, likewise "selected a variety of the most approved Novels, of the most approved authors" for his library. Although they stocked "best" novels, few proprietors felt constrained to protect their patrons' "right to read"; Angell, for example, pledging "himself to consign to the flames, every work of the latter description [e.g., novels], which savors in the least of an immoral tendency, when painted [sic] out."[9]

Some early circulating library proprietors protested

that their establishments did not deserve reputations as "slop-shops in literature." Joseph Osborn of New York hoped in 1805 "to convince those of their error who imagine that Novels and Romances constitute the principal part of his collection."[10] Fully four-fifths of his fellow proprietors before 1810 could have made similar claims about their own holdings since collections to that time tended to be quite diverse. Neither of the two popular generalizations regarding circulating libraries was warranted; women were not the only persons served by the early circulating libraries, nor were their stocks solely or even predominantly fiction in those early years. Since these were, however, the two areas of most significant innovation for the circulating libraries, they were, as is the fate of any innovator, obliged to suffer society's disapprobation for their efforts as well as its patronage.

The contributions of American circulating libraries were not limited, however, to serving women and supplying popular literature. They were responsible also for the widespread introduction into library practice of three other new departures. These were: (1) the supplying of newspapers, periodicals, and ephemeral pamphlets; (2) the maintenance of extended hours of opening; and (3) the provision of on-site reading facilities. These three services cannot be considered innovations, however, because they were not truly new; they were rather adapted out of the coffeehouses, where they had already in a sense been available for several decades.

These three interrelated library activities had risen out of eighteenth-century society's growing need for current intelligences on mercantile, political, and social matters. The newspapers and periodicals that came into being to provide such current information, however, did not lend themselves easily to the long-standing library practice of opening up weekly to charge their materials out to patrons to be read elsewhere. Newspapers and other periodicals needed rather to be available only briefly but to many patrons throughout the day while their contents were still of current significance. The coffeehouses had been able, during an interim period, to accommodate this need relatively well, but by the latter decades of the eighteenth century the volume of such literature was larger than they could effectively manage, and the circulating libraries were the first to provide more appropriately for it.

Just as the coffeehouses, so also could the circulating libraries remain open throughout the day, since they were usually operated in tandem with another business, often a bookstore, and had to incur therefore no additional staffing, heating, or lighting costs to do so. From Colonial times they thus maintained extended hours of service, a practice which other kinds of libraries could not afford in most communities to adopt for several decades thereafter.

Not only were the hours of service in the eighteenth-century social and academic libraries largely limited to one or two brief periods weekly, but for the most part they also lacked on-site accommodations for readers. Here again the circulating libraries were usually able first to assume the community responsibility for such facilities. Reading accommodations could hardly be justified in the social libraries which were open only a couple of hours weekly, but a few chairs could be easily made available throughout the week in a circulating library where the fireplace and lamps were already lit for the attendant proprietor-cum-bookseller.

The availability of these three services in the circulating libraries, all well-established by the turn of the nineteenth century, did much to create the expectation in the public mind that other kinds of libraries in the community ought to be able to serve similarly. The atheneums, which began in Boston in 1807 and spread during the subsequent two decades to a number of other larger and wealthier cities, adopted all three services as their regular stock in trade. The Boston Athenaeum, however, offered nothing to its members that Caritat had not provided to the subscribers to his Literary Assembly in New York several years earlier. Most atheneums eventually merged with social libraries, which in turn gave way in the latter half of the century to free public libraries. By then extended hours, reading accommodations, and current materials had become standard services in public libraries.

Another innovation pioneered by the circulating libraries was what would today be called "out-reach" service. Home delivery of books, always available under special circumstances from the circulating libraries, became for some a standard, advertised activity in several locations in the 1850s and 1860s and continued in some cases right into the twentieth century.[11] This motivation to bring books to readers wherever they were, profit-inspired though it may have been, also prompted some commercial libraries to begin in the 1860s to establish branch outlets, another initiative followed later by the public libraries.

The public libraries seem never to have attempted to follow the lead of the rental chains in the 1920s and 1930s in placing small bookracks widely throughout their communities; apparently that, along with home and office delivery, constituted "reaching out" a little too far. The public libraries did, however, eventually take over the entire basic rationale of the circulating libraries when they began themselves in the 1910s to rent books to readers for a fee.

It seems clear that much of the durability of the circulating libraries must have resulted from their willingness to initiate new library services, initiatives which in most cases came later to be adopted into the standard practices of most other kinds of libraries.

Economic Advantages of the Circulating Libraries

The circulating libraries also enjoyed a number of economic advantages over their contemporary institutions. A few have already been mentioned, such as the fact that they could remain open through extended hours and maintain reading accommodations usually at small if any supernumerary costs. They had other advantages as well, not the least of which was that being open many hours per week enabled them to gain more rapid turnover in their rental stocks than could libraries that only exchanged books weekly.

Also working to the benefit of the circulating libraries was the fact that they were most often conjoined with bookstores, giving them substantial manipulatability in their rental holdings. They could with ease move books from their sale shelves to their circulating shelves and back again in accord with the slightest shift in public taste. Being commercial establishments they could also buy or barter books from their customers to replenish their shelves. This ability to modify their circulating collections kept their shelves more attractive than those of the other lending libraries of the time where collections remained more rigidly fixed.

It was also to the circulating libraries' advantage that most of them operated in prime commercial locations. Furthermore, being in the book-trade, they were able to obtain discount rates on their purchases which were in most cases unavailable to other kinds of libraries. Also, although the circulating and social libraries generally maintained competitive subscription rates, the commercial libraries were almost always prepared to rent by-the-book, thereby obviating the need for a patron to raise the full annual fee before he could read; this concession seems seldom to have been made in the social libraries.

And finally, it must have accrued to the economic advantage of the commercial libraries that they were usually operated by professional bookmen, where the other libraries of the time were not. These bookmen, usually bred to the trade, were often able to provide a larger share of the literary leadership in their communities than could the custodians of most contemporary social libraries. They could usually discuss books, advise on reading, select stocks, and maintain services more knowledgeably than could their counterparts in other kinds of libraries. This advantage began to diminish, however, in the middle of the nineteenth century and had probably faded completely from the scene by 1900 as more and more public librarians began coming trained to their posts. For more than a century, however, it had been a condition of benefit to the circulating libraries.

Disadvantages for the Circulating Libraries

Probably the major disadvantage for the circulating libraries during their first hundred years in America was that they were seldom able to command the prestige of the social libraries. There was never anything exclusive about the circulating libraries; anyone with sixpence in his pocket could borrow a book for a week. Social libraries, on the other hand, being clubs of individuals banded together to acquire a book collection in common, had an elitist appeal which few circulating libraries could match. Caritat was probably able to match it; perhaps also were Callendar, Hammond, Brotherhead, Robinson, and a few others. But in general prestige seems to have been an advantage enjoyed by the social libraries.

And of course the biggest advantage of all held by public libraries after the middle of the nineteenth century was their tax support. There was no way that the circulating libraries could compete head-to-head with free libraries. They managed to survive thereafter entirely by providing, for a fee, services which the public libraries could not, or would not, provide free. For the most part this meant that they held the market for a service only for a period of time, because in most cases the public libraries came soon to dispense the very same service gratis, forcing the commercial libraries to move into still other areas where the public libraries were not yet prepared to go. For a fee they filled the interstices of free library service, as it were, on ad interim bases, until society became willing to assume their cost into the growing array of tax-supported library activities.

It perhaps stands as mute testimony to the boundless ingenuity inspired by the profit incentive that after more than two centuries of this continuing process, commercial library services remain today an active segment of the library industry in the United States. Or perhaps that is not the point at all. Perhaps this centuries-old process rather bespeaks the inexorable absorptive character of library services in a democracy; perhaps libraries have such an integral function in a democracy that any service, once its social utility has been proven, must of necessity be made available to all citizens regardless of their ability to pay for it. There are likely for a long time to come to be adherents to both views.

REFERENCES

1. *Baltimore Federal Gazette*, September 27, 1809.
2. Epithets coined respectively for circulating libraries by Elizabeth Griffith in her preface to *Lady Barton* (1771) and by Richard Brinsley Sheridan in *The Rivals* (1775).

3. "Essays," *Boston Weekly Magazine* 1 (January 22, 1803): 53.

4. Susanna Rowson, *Mentoria*, 2 vols. (Philadelphia: Robert Campbell, 1794), 2: 87.

5. "Novel Reading a Cause of Female Depravity." *Monthly Mirror* 4 (November 1797): 277-79. This essay was reprinted in the *New England Quarterly* in 1802.

6. The *Detroit Free Press,* as late as June 10, 1877 told for example of a young woman "of fine education, who gratified a vitiated taste for novel reading till her reason was over-thrown, and she has, in consequence, been for several years an inmate of an insane asylum."

7. John Dabney, *Catalogue of Books, for Sale or Circulation* . . . ([Salem]: Printed for J. Dabney, 1791), Preface.

8. *Baltimore Federal Gazette,* September 5, 1809.

9. *Warren* (R.I.) *Clarion,* March 27, 1824.

10. "Literary Intelligence," *Port Folio* 5 (September 7, 1805): 277.

11. See, for example, "The Roving Library of Vesta Eales," *Publishers' Weekly* 138 (July 20, 1940): 162-63.

Checklist of American Commercial Library Enterprises, 1762-1890

The following list of circulating libraries does not purport to be complete. It is rather an enumeration of those circulating libraries which were come upon in the preparation of this study. Hopefully other investigators will add to this list as a step toward the ultimate development of a complete census of such institutions. The author would appreciate being cited to other American circulating libraries and commercial reading rooms that existed between 1762 and 1890.

In almost all cases, the following entries include citations to the sources whence they came. Complete bibliographical information on these sources is given in the appended list of references. Where a source is not identified herein, the information was taken from the respective library catalogue. These catalogues are listed in Appendix I.

William Aikman's Circulating Library, which was established in 1773 in Annapolis, Md., contained some 1,200 volumes [Moore]

Albion Library, 13 Park Street in New York, was taken over by B. Taylor, the City Surveyor, in 1808 from James Osborn and was continued for three years thereafter [Raddin's *Hocquet Caritat*, McKay]

Allen's Circulating Library of Providence, R.I., was established in 1871; by 1876 it contained a thousand volumes and was earning $400 annually [USBE *Public Libraries*]

Allen & Cowens' Circulating Library in Palmer, Mass., held 500 volumes in 1876 and circulated 2,500 books per year for a gross annual income of $212 [USBE *Public Libraries*]

Allis' Circulating Library (Birmingham, Conn.) was established in 1854; its published catalogue of 1887 [?] listed some 4,000 volumes [USBE *Report*]

Allis' Circulating Library (Derby, Conn.), which was founded in 1854, reported a collection comprising 2,500 volumes in 1876 [USBE *Public Libraries*]

American Eclectic Library was established in New York City in 1869; its 30,300 volumes were lent out 52,000 times in 1876 [USBE *Public Libraries*]

Amesbury (Mass.) Circulating Library, founded in 1868, reported holding 850 volumes eight years later when it was circulating some 8,500 books annually [USBE *Public Libraries*]

W. P. Andrew, see Union Library (Phenix, R.I.)

Samuel Angell's Circulating Library of Warren, R.I., was purchased from Stephen Davol in 1824 and was still in business in 1826 [Browns' *R.I.*]

Anger's Circulating Library in Milwaukee contained 3,000 volumes in 1857 [Rhees]

Annapolis (Md.) Circulating Library was established by Stephen Clark, bookseller, stationer and bookbinder in Church Street; it contained about 1,500 volumes and issued a catalogue in 1783 [Moore, Evans]

William Aplin's Reading Room functioned as part of his bookstore and publishing office in Providence, R.I., between 1836 and 1844 [Browns' *R.I.*]

George O. Arnold's Circulating Library, Providence, R.I., was established in 1853 in his printing office, periodical dealership, and fancy goods store; it contained 2,000 volumes in 1876 [Browns' *R.I.*, USBE *Public Libraries*]

W. H. Attree, see Irving Circulating Library (New York)

Auburn (N.Y.) Circulating Library contained 800 volumes in 1816 [Hamilton]

Thomas A. Baird's Circulating Library, which he opened in Washington, Pa., in 1811, continued in business for at least two years [Crumrine, Forrest]

Luke Baker's Circulating Library, Boston, was opened in 1813 at 69 Court Street, where it remained for at least eight years [Silver's *Boston*]

Stephens Baker's Circulating Library in Beverly, Mass., was founded in 1842 [Stone]

T. M. Baker's Circulating Library, 24 Main Street in Boston, claimed 2,500 volumes in 1819; it was continuing in business in 1821 [Shera]

Charles N. Baldwin's Circulating Library was part of his bookselling operation at 106 Chatham Street in New York City in 1811 [McKay]

Baltimore Circulating Library, which was opened in 1793, was being maintained by William Munday in 1800 and was continued by him to his death nineteen years later, at which time it was taken over by Lucy L. Hunter; it issued catalogues and supplements in 1793, 1802, 1807, 1809, and 1812 [Silver's *Baltimore*, Moore, Evans]

Baltimore Reading Rooms at 204 Market Street, were opened by Coale & Maxwell in 1815 [Silver's *Baltimore*]

Barclay Library, supposedly a commercial lending library in Brookville, Pa., existed in 1857 [Rhees]

Hugh Barkley's Circulating Library was purchased from William Murphy of Baltimore in 1786 and contained 2,490 volumes a year later [Moore]

William Barlas' Circulating Library was bought from Alexander Somerville of New York in 1800 and was continued by Barlas for a decade [Raddin's *Hocquet Caritat*, McKay]

Samuel Barnes, see Fell's Point Circulating Library

Barnes & Co.'s Circulating Library was opened in La Salle, Ill., in 1875; the following year it had 450 volumes in its collections which it lent 1,500 times, earning therefrom $250 [USBE *Public Libraries*]

Bartholomew's Select Library in New Haven, Conn., was opened in 1871, issued a 33-page catalogue the following year, and reported containing 3,000 volumes in 1876 [USBE *Public Libraries*]

Samuel Bartlett's Circulating Library was located at 78 Bowery in New York City in 1819-1820 [McKay]

Wilson Baxter, see Fitchburg Circulating Library

Ephraim C. Beals' Circulating Library was located at 58 Middle Street in Boston in 1809 [Silver's *Boston*; see also Franklin Circulating Library (Boston)]

A. S. Beckwith, see Robinson & Beckwith's Circulating Library

Robert Bell, see Universal Circulating Library

James D. Bemis' Circulating Library was established in his bookstore in Canandaigua, N. Y., in 1819 [McKelvey]

Bend City Circulating Library in California was in business in 1864 [Held]

Stephen G. Benedict, see Pawtucket Reading Room

Benicia Circulating Library was maintained in the Pioneer Cheap Cash Grocery in Benicia, Cal., in the early 1870s [Held]

Bennett Library was reportedly a commercial lending library established in Kingston, Pa., in 1851; it contained 1,000 volumes six years later [Rhees]

Samuel Berrian's Circulating Library was located at 35 Chatham Street in New York when it issued a catalogue in 1803 but at 19 Fair Street during the subsequent five years [McKay, Shaw]

Biddeford (Me.) Circulating Library contained 600 volumes which it circulated 6,188 times in 1876, earning $520 [USBE *Public Libraries*]

Nathaniel P. Bixley, see Maryland Circulating Library

William Blagrove, see Union Circulating Library (Boston)

George E. Blake's Circulating Library was operated in connection with his music store in Philadelphia, first at 1 South Third from 1803 to 1814 and then at 13 South Fifth until 1823 when it was purchased and merged into Joseph Robinson's library in Baltimore [Silver's *Baltimore,* Moore]

William P. Blake's Circulating Library was located in New York City when its catalogue was published in 1818 [See also Boston Circulating Library]

David P. Bliss' Circulating Library was operated in conjunction with his bookbindery at 235 Greenwich Street in New York City in 1814 and 1815 [McKay]

Edmund Blunt's Circulating Library in his bookshop on State Street in Newburyport, Mass., contained 1,500 volumes in 1798; it was sold in 1803 to William Sawyer and Edward Little [Shera]

John A. Boeller's Circulating Library in Evansville, Ind., founded in 1872, contained 3,300 volumes four years later [USBE *Public Libraries*]

A. L. Boimare's Circulating Library in New Orleans had its own reading room in 1825 and claimed to possess 10,000 volumes seven years later [McCutcheon, Tinker]

William Bonnel's Circulating Library was located on Chestnut Street in Philadelphia between 1795 and 1817 [Brown's *Philadelphia*]

Book Exchange of Washington, D.C., was a kind of commercial library; in 1876 its 10,000 volumes circulated 7,000 times [USBE *Public Libraries*]

Boston Circulating Library was opened by William Martin in 1785 at 45 Main Street, but he discontinued the effort two years later; he issued a catalogue in 1786 [Evans, Bolton]

Boston Circulating Library was taken over from Benjamin Guild's estate in 1792 by William P. Blake, who sold it fourteen years later to bookbinder William Andrews; in 1808 it was taken over by Elias Penniman, Jr., who eventually sold it to Charles Metcalf [Bolton, Silver's *Boston*]

Boston Union Circulating Library, see Union Circulating Library (Boston)

Bouchon's Circulating Library was in operation in New Orleans in 1817 [McCutcheon]

John Boyd's Circulating Library of 500 volumes in Pittsburgh may never have got beyond the proposal issued in 1788 [Wright/Corbett]

Boylston Circulating Library, which was located at No. 90, Newbury Street in Boston in 1820, produced a catalogue of its contents in 1837 [Silver's *Boston*]

H. P. Bradbury, see Post Meridian Reading Room

Thomas Bradford's Circulating Library in Philadelphia, which issued a catalogue in 1769, was still in operation four years later [Lamberton, Bridenbaugh's *Rebels*, Evans]

Widow Bradish's Circulating Library was located at 124 Broadway in New York City in 1811 [McKay]

Brooklyn (N.Y.) Circulating Library, located "at the office of the Long-Island Star, Fulton Street," issued a catalogue in 1821 [Shoemaker]

William Brotherhead's Circulating Library was

founded in Philadelphia in 1861 and contained some 35,000 volumes fifteen years later [USBE *Public Libraries*, Brotherhead]

John C. Brown's Circulating Library was in business in Greenwich, R.I., in 1855/56 [Browns' *R.I.*]

Brown's Circulating Library was established in 1866 in Stroudsburg, Pa.; it reported to the U.S. Bureau of Education Report of 1876 that it then owned 500 volumes, which it had lent out 1,200 times during the year gaining therefrom a total income of $100 [USBE *Public Libraries*]

Joseph T. Buckingham, see Theological Circulating Library (Boston)

Buckingham (Conn.) Circulating Library reported holding 450 volumes in 1876 [USBE *Public Libraries*]

John N. Burgess' Circulating Library was located in his bookstore at 125 Hope in Bristol, R.I. in 1858 [Browns' *R.I.*]

Burley Bros.' Circulating Library in Chicago was purchased from Stephen F. Gale in the mid-1840s [Spencer]

Thomas Burnham's Circulating Library was located at 58 Cornhill in Boston in 1830 [Bolton]

Keziah Butler's Circulating Library was operated in conjunction with her millinery shop at several locations in Boston between 1804 and 1825 or after [Silver's *Boston*]

A. A. Call, see Phoenix Circulating Library

Charles Callendar, see Shakspeare Circulating Library

Cambridge Circulating Library, operating out of the University Bookstore on Harvard Square, published a catalogue in 1861.

James Campbell's Circulating Library, located in the Museum Building at 18 Tremont Street in Boston, issued a catalogue of its holdings in 1870.

Hocquet Caritat's Circulating Library was taken over from John Fellows of New York in 1797 and, following the issuing of several catalogues, was disposed of to John Osborn in 1804 [McKay, Raddin's *Hocquet Caritat*]

Carrington Library of Cumberland, Pa., which reported holding 2,500 volumes in 1857, appears to have been intended as a profit-making venture [Rhees]

Mary Carroll's Reading Room was serving a New Orleans clientele in 1830 [McCutcheon]

Cassell's Library of Harleysville, Pa., founded in 1835, reported 8,000 volumes in 1857 and 10,750 in 1876 [Rhees, USBE *Public Libraries*]

Centinel Circulating Library was operating in Newark, N.J., in 1807 [Sabine]

Central Circulating Library (Boston) was operated by Mayhew & Baker at 208 Washington Street; it issued a catalogue in 1860.

Central Circulating Library (Salem, Mass.) was run by Hannah Harris in the early 1820s when it contained some 4,000 volumes [Tapley]

Central Circulating Library (Springfield, Mass.) claimed to have 1,200 volumes in 1876 and to enjoy a gross annual income of $1,000; it was founded in 1867 [USBE *Public Libraries*]

Central Square Circulating Library in Malden, Mass., was four years old in 1876, when it reportedly had 1,250 volumes [USBE *Public Libraries*]

John Chalk's Circulating Library in his "musical repository" in Philadelphia between 1796 and 1802 is said to have contained 2,000 volumes [Browns' *Philadelphia*]

Chamberlain's Circulating Library in Worcester, Mass., claimed in 1876 to have 2,500 volumes and to circulate 17,000 books annually for an income of $1,375 [USBE *Public Libraries*]

Chambers' Loan Library in Morrisville, N.Y., contained 500 volumes in 1876, which was its eighth year of operation [USBE *Public Libraries*]

Champaign County Circulating Library was opened in 1858 at Hunt, Sim & Co.'s Drug & Bookstore in Urbana, Ill. [Eaton]

Aristarchus Champion's Circulating Library, established in Chagrin Falls, Ohio, in 1847, reportedly comprised 800 volumes [Stiffler]

Joseph Charless' Coffee House Reading Room in Louisville, Ky., was proposed in 1807 [Kaser's *Charless*; see also *Missouri Gazette* Reading Room]

Charleston Circulating Library gave 114 volumes to the new Charleston, Ill., Public Library about 1901 [Sharp]

Charlestown (Mass.) Circulating Library produced a 56-page catalogue of its collections in 1819 [Shaw]

George Charter's Circulating Library in New York City issued a catalogue in 1817.

George Charter's Circulating Library in Cincinnati was operated out of his bookstore between 1818 and 1824 [Sutton]

City Circulating Library (St. Louis, Mo.) was opened by R. Jones Woodward at 32 Chestnut Street in 1842 and soon claimed to own 10,000 volumes [Eaton]

Ambrose Clark's Circulating Library was proposed in Baltimore in 1789 [Moore]

Clark & Austin's Circulating Library was opened in Anaheim, Cal., in 1873 [Held]

Joseph Clendenin's Circulating Library was maintained in his bookstore in Lancaster, Pa., during the period up to 1811 [Ellis/Evans]

Coale & Maxwell, see Baltimore Reading Rooms

Cobb's Library, on Washington Street near State in Chicago, was founded in 1869; in spite of severe losses in the Great Fire, it had grown to more than 9,000 volumes by 1876; it was discontinued in 1894 [Spencer, Sharp, USBE *Public Libraries*]

Aaron Coe & M. Ward's Circulating Library was opened at the Sign of Franklin's Head in Newark, N.J. in 1802 [Sabine]

Coggeshall's Circulating Library, which was opened in Lowell, Mass., in 1874, claimed to have 500 volumes in 1876; it circulated 5,000 books and grossed $250 per year [USBE *Public Libraries*]

Cohoes (N.Y.) Circulating Library contained 800 volumes in 1876 [USBE *Public Libraries*]

Cole & Eddy's Circulating Library was operated in conjunction with their bookselling, periodical dealership, and ice-cream store in Warren, R.I., between 1858 and the conclusion of the Civil War [Browns' *R.I.*]

Benjamin Coleman's Circulating Library was maintained in Salem, Mass., between 1832 and 1837 [Shera]

Coleman & Chisholm's Circulating Library in Portland, Me., issued three catalogues during the early 1830s [Shera]

R. Colton, see Franklin Circulating Library (Woodstock, Vt.)

Commonwealth Circulating Library in Boston claimed in 1876 to own some 1,800 volumes and to be circulating approximately 26,000 books annually [USBE *Public Libraries*]

John Cook's Reading Room, where he also sold Saratoga Spring water, was in operation in Albany, N.Y., before 1820 [Tolman]

Charles G. Cornell's Circulating Library was maintained in his book and newspaper stand in the LaGrange, Ind., post office in 1887 [Curless]

John Corson's Circulating Library was opened in 1813 in his bookstore on Main Street in Cincinnati [Sutton]

Cottom & Stewart's Circulating Library operated in Fredericksburg, Va., for about a decade beginning in 1803 [Moore]

Edward J. Cowell, see Peoria (Ill.) Circulating Library

Zadok Cramer's Circulating Library of some 1,000 volumes was founded in Pittsburgh in 1801; it was merged with other collections in 1814 to form the "Pittsburgh Permanent Library" [Wright/Corbett]

John Creery, see Theological Library (Baltimore, Md.)

Crosswell Circulating Library was doing business in New Haven, Conn., in the 1840s [Shera]

Culbertson Library in Danville, Ill., founded in 1867, grossed $2,000 from its 1,250-volume collection in 1876 [USBE *Public Libraries*]

Henry Cushing's Circulating Library, "at the sign of the Bible and Anchor" in Providence, issued a catalogue in 1800 [Evans]

Isaac Cushing's Circulating Library existed in Fitchburg, Mass., in the early 1830s [Shera]

Cushing & Appleton, see Essex Circulating Library (Salem, Mass.)

John Dabney's Circulating Library was opened in Salem, Mass., in 1789; it issued catalogues in 1791, 1794, and 1801, and it continued in business until 1819 [Tapley, Shaw]

Daily American Reading Room in Nashville, Tenn., was in operation in 1848 [Kaser's *Coffee House*]

Daily Circulating Library of East Attleboro, Mass., after three years of operation, claimed some 300 volumes; it circulated 2,200 books annually, however, grossing a reported $200, of which $130 went for new books [USBE *Public Libraries*]

George Dana, see Perrin's Circulating Library

Benjamin Davenport, see Franklin Circulating Library (Boston)

Matthew Davenport's Circulating Library, in his fabrics shop in Cumberland, R.I., dates from 1805 [Browns' *R.I.*]

Davis & Force, see Washington Circulating Library

Stephen Davol's Circulating Library in Warren, R.I., was purchased by Samuel Angell in 1824 [Browns' *R.I.*]

George E. H. Day, see Painesville (Ohio) Circulating Library

Nathaniel Dearborn, see Providence Cheapside Circulating Library

Dearth & Sterry's Circulating Library (Golden Dearth and Erastus Sterry) was conducted in their printing and bookselling establishment in Warren, R.I., in 1808 [Browns' *R.I.*]

Decker & Dyer's Reading Room was operated in connection with their soda fountain in Nashville, Tenn., for at least three years beginning in 1825 [Kaser's *Coffee House*]

Denison & Burdick's Circulating Library in Elgin, Ill., sold out its 700 volumes for $500 to the newly-established Public Library there in 1874 [Sharp]

Richard Denmore's Circulating Library was opened in 1801 in Washington, D.C. [Noble]

Denver's Library in Sacramento, Cal., in 1857 appears to have been a commercial venture [Rhees]

Dickerman's Circulating Library in Taunton, Mass., reported a circulation of 10,000 in 1876 from its collection of 2,000 volumes [USBE *Public Libraries*]

Jacob D. Dietrick's Circulating Library in Hagerstown, Md., issued a 98-page list of its holdings in 1801 [Shaw]

Bernard Dornin, see Roman Catholic Library

Dowe's Circulating Library in West Killingly, Conn., contained 800 volumes in 1876, some fourteen years after its establishment [USBE *Public Libraries*]

Nicholas Dufief's Circulating Library was maintained in Philadelphia during the first two decades of the nineteenth century [Browns' *Philadelphia*]

Henry Dury's Circulating Library in Cincinnati was located at 121 Main Street in 1830 [Sutton]

Edgington (Ill.) Circulating Library owned 400 volumes in 1857 [Rhees]

Hubbard Edmands & Co.'s Circulating Library was operated out of their City Bookstore in Indianapolis following 1834 [Dunn's *Indianapolis*]

Elizabeth (N.J.) Circulating Library, founded in 1862, circulated its 586 books 5,000 times in 1876, accruing an income therefrom of $350 [USBE *Public Libraries*]

Ellis' Circulating Library in New Orleans published a catalogue as early as 1841; in 1876 it claimed that its 9,000 volumes circulated 150,000 times annually [USBE *Public Libraries*]

Emerson & Stott, see West Side Library

Z. Ernst & Sons' Reading Room, operating in conjunction with their brewery in Cincinnati in 1819, offered files of fifty American and English newspapers [Martin]

Essex Circulating Library (Newburyport, Mass.) was operated by printer/bookseller Angier March in 1803 [Shera]

Essex Circulating Library (Salem, Mass.) was established by Cushing & Appleton in 1814 and was run by John M. Ives from 1821 to 1835; its catalogues of 1818, 1822, and

1826 show collections ranging between 3,000 and 5,000 volumes [Tapley]

Fairfield (Me.) Circulating Library comprised 300 volumes in 1876 [USBE *Public Libraries*]

Fairhaven (Mass.) Circulating Library was operating before 1800 [Shera]

Caroline H. Fanning's Circulating Library was located on School Street in Boston in 1816 [Silver's *Boston*]

Farmington (N.H.) Circulating Library held 420 volumes in 1876, which it loaned 4,000 times that year, accruing $325 income therefrom [USBE *Public Libraries*]

Fayette Library of Hillsdale, Mich., which was founded in 1851, claimed to possess 400 volumes in 1857 [Rhees]

John Fellows' Circulating Library, in operation in New Lork City between 1793 and 1797, issued a catalogue in 1796 [McKay, Raddin's *Hocquet Caritat*, Evans]

Fellows & Simpson's Circulating Library of 200 volumes was situated in their bookstore in Belfast, Me., between its establishment in 1824 and its sale five years later to Noyes P. Hawes; it reportedly contained 600 volumes at time of sale [Shera]

Fell's Point (Md.) Circulating Library was operated from 1808 to 1810 by Samuel Barnes in his bookstore, issuing at least two catalogues during that time [Silver's *Baltimore*]

John Fernagus' Circulating Library was located in his bookstore in Philadelphia during the second decade of the nineteenth century [Browns' *Philadelphia*]

C.M.S. Fessenden's Circulating Library was operated in conjunction with his bookselling establishment in Warren, R.I., in 1856 [Browns' *R.I.*]

G. M. Fessenden, see Franklin Circulating Library (Warren, R.I.)

Fetterman's Circulating Library in Kansas City, Mo., had 1,300 volumes in 1876 and was still in business eight years later [USBE *Public Libraries*]

Fitchburg Circulating Library in Massachusetts was operated successively between 1830 and 1835 by Wilson Baxter, Whitcomb & Cook, and W. S. Wilder [Shera]

O. W. Flanders, see Haverhill Circulating Library

Foreign Library, No.13 West Street in Boston, operated in the 1840s by Elizabeth Peabody, contained some 300 works in French and fewer volumes in German, Italian, and Spanish [Stern's *Books*]

Samuel Foss' Circulating Library in Woonsocket, R.I., was offered for sale in 1861 [Browns' *R.I.*]

Adams Foster's Circulating Library in Providence, R.I., may never really have existed in his name; Foster was a coal dealer in 1836 when he offered S. T. Thurber's Circulating Library of 4,000 volumes for sale [Browns' *R.I.*]

Foster, Drown & Co.'s Circulating Library opened in Providence in 1789 [Browns' *R.I.*]

Franklin Circulating Library (Boston) at 67 Court Street, was operated by Benjamin Davenport from 1820 to 1825 [Silver's *Boston*]

Franklin Circulating Library (Danvers, Mass.) was under the proprietorship of Amos Trask, Jr. when it issued its catalogue in 1834.

Franklin Circulating Library (Providence, R.I.) was maintained in 1852 by Parkhurst & Brother in their book and music store at 47 Westminster [Browns' *R.I.*]

Franklin Circulating Library (St. Louis, Mo.) was opened by S. W. Meech in 1833 at his bookstore [*Missouri Republican,* January 1, 1833]

Franklin Circulating Library (Warren, R.I.) was maintained between 1831 and 1845 by G. M. Fessenden [Browns' *R.I.*]

Franklin Circulating Library (Woodstock, Vt.) was established in 1828 by R. Colton and absorbed later into Haskell's Circulating Library [Shera]

Franklin Library (Camden, N.J.), in business in 1857, appears to have been a library operated for profit [Rhees]

Franklin Library (Pawtucket, R.I.) was operating under the oversight of R. Horton, bookseller, in 1847 [Browns' *R.I.*]

Franklin Library (Washington, Ohio), which was in business in 1857, appears to have been intended to return a profit to its proprietors [Rhees]

Donald Fraser's Circulating Library was maintained in connection with his bookstore on William Street in New York for more than a decade following 1802 [Raddin's *Hocquet Caritat*, McKay]

French Circulating Library was operated by Joseph de la Grange of Philadelphia between 1797 and 1799 [Browns' *Philadelphia*]

French's Circulating Library in Lewiston, Me., held 2,180 volumes which it circulated 12,000 times in 1876 for a gross earning of $800; it had been established six years earlier [USBE *Public Libraries*]

Benjamin Franklin French's Reading Room was maintained in New Orleans between 1842 and 1847 [Maestri]

Jacob Frieze's Reading Room (Pawtucket, R.I.) was opened in 1831 [Browns' *R.I.*]

Jacob Frieze's Reading Room (Providence, R.I.) was operating in 1833 [Browns' *R.I.*]

Carl Fuelling's Circulating Library in St. Joseph, Mo., was established in 1867; nine years later it reportedly grossed $500 from its 6,000-volume collection [USBE *Public Libraries*]

J. Gadsby, see Indian Queen Tavern Reading Room

Stephen F. Gale's Circulating Library was in business in Chicago in 1836; it contained about 1,600 volumes ten years later, near the time that it was sold to Burley Bros. [Spencer]

Frank Gay's Circulating Library was located in his bookstore at 140 Westminster in Providence, R.I., during the Civil War [Browns' *R.I.*]

General Circulating Library in Philadelphia was operated by Lewis Nicola for a couple of years following 1769 [Lamberton, Bridenbaugh's *Rebels*]

German Circulating Library in Philadelphia, was maintained in Fourth Street between Race and Vine by Jacob Lahn; it had over 1,000 volumes of "the best German authors" in 1785, but it closed a year or two later [Browns' *Philadelphia*, Knauss]

Samuel Gifford's Circulating Library, established in

Charleston, S.C., in 1772, appears to have been short-lived [Moore]

John Gilkison's Circulating Library was established in his Pittsburgh bookstore about 1798 [Wright's *Culture*]

Caleb Gill, Jr's., Circulating Library in Hingham, Mass., possessed "upward of 500 volumes" in 1827 [Shera]

Gill & Hayes' Circulating Library was established in Springfield, Mass., in 1871; it had 1,200 volumes five years later and circulated 16,500 books for a gross income of $450 per annum, of which it reported spending $300 for books and $300 for salaries [sic] [USBE *Public Libraries*]

W. & J. Gilman, see Merrimac Circulating Library

Gledhill & Cady's Circulating Library was opened in Chattanooga, Tenn., in 1873; in 1876 it owned 400 volumes and earned an income of $125 [USBE *Public Libraries*]

J. C. Good & Co.'s Circulating Library of Massillon, Ohio, contained 309 volumes in 1876, which it lent 1,710 times that year grossing $150 income; the library had been opened two years earlier [USBE *Public Libraries*]

A. T. Goodrich & Co.'s Circulating Library, located at the corner of Broadway and Cedar Streets in New York, produced a catalogue in 1818.

Goodsen's Circulating Library in Bellevue, Ohio, contained 500 volumes in 1876 [USBE *Public Libraries*]

E. B. Gould's Circulating Library moved in 1810 from Newark, N. J. to Greenwich, N. Y. [Sabine]

R. S. Gould's Circulating Library was located opposite the hotel in Pawtucket, Rhode Island in 1832-33 [Browns' *R.I.*]

Joseph de la Grange, see French Circulating Library

John Gray, Jr., see Phoenix Circulating Library

William Fairfax Gray's Circulating Library in Fredericksburg, Va., was founded in 1822 and continued in business for about a year [Moore]

Griggsville (Ill.) Circulating Library, opened in 1869, held 900 volumes seven years later [Sharp, USBE *Public Libraries*]

Benjamin Guild's Circulating Library was maintained at 59 Cornhill in Boston from 1785 until 1792 when it passed from his estate to William P. Blake; it issued catalogues in 1788, 1789, and 1790 [Bolton]

Guilford Circulating Library in Connecticut, also known as *Shepard & Fowler's*, existed between 1872 and 1907; its annual circulation of 5,000 from a collection of 625 volumes brought in $175 in 1875 [USBE *Public Libraries*]

Hallowell (Me.) Circulating Library published a 48-page catalogue of its holdings in 1820 [Shoemaker]

H. J. Hamilton's Circulating Library and periodical depot in Central Falls, R.I., existed in 1854 [Browns' *R.I.*]

James Hammond's Circulating Library of Newport, R.I., was acquired by him from Wanton & Rathburn of Providence in 1811; in 1852 Hammond claimed that its 8,000 volumes made it the largest circulating library in New England, although by 1860 it had grown to 10,000 [Browns' *R.I.*, Shera]

John T. Hanzsche's Circulating Library was located at 30 Baltimore Street in Baltimore in 1840 [Moore]

Isaac W. Harper's Circulating Library was established in Reading, Pa., in 1840 [Palmer-Poroner]

Harper Library in Lewiston Falls, Me., in 1857 seems to have been a commercial library [Rhees]

Hannah Harris, see Central Circulating Library (Salem, Mass.)

Henry Hart's Circulating Library and bookstore were located at 117 Chatham Street in New York in 1809 [McKay]

Hart's Circulating Library of Providence, R.I., was advertised in 1810 [Browns' *R.I.*]

Hartford Circulating Library in Connecticut was sixteen years old when it reported holding 4,500 volumes in 1876 [USBE *Public Libraries*]

John E. Harwood's Circulating Library at 75 North Third Street in Philadelphia issued a catalogue of its holdings in 1803.

Haskell's Circulating Library of Woodstock, Vt., was bought by Nahum Haskell from Charles Henry and Isaac

N. Cushman; although Haskell died in 1867, the library was still in business in 1889 [Shera]

William Hastings, see Waterville (Me.) Circulating Library

Haverhill Circulating Library (Mass.) was owned by O. W. Flanders in 1857, when it reported holding 600 volumes; it issued a catalogue in 1855 [Rhees]

E. M. Hawes Circulating Library of Woonsocket, R.I., was purchased from A. S. Streeter in 1834 and was operated thereafter with his lottery office [Browns' *R.I.*]

Noyes P. Hawes' Circulating Library of Belfast, Me., was reported to contain about 600 volumes when he purchased it from Fellows & Simpson in 1829 [Shera]

Hawkins' Circulating Library opened in Brooklyn with 400 volumes in 1848; within a quarter century it had built up a multilingual fiction stock of some 17,000 volumes which were lent out between 20,000 and 25,000 times per year [USBE *Public Libraries*]

C. A. Haydock's Circulating Library was operating out of his bookstore in Newark, N.J., in 1827 [Sabine]

Henry & Cushman's Circulating Library in Woodstock, Vt., was opened in 1821 by Charles Henry and Isaac N. Cushman; they sold it later to Nahum Haskell [Shera]

Hill & Gittings' Circulating Library of Carrollton, Mo., reported owning 600 volumes in 1876 [USBE *Public Libraries*]

John H. Hinch's Circulating Library and newspaper depot was located at 156 South Main Street in Providence, R.I., in 1865 [Browns' *R.I.*]

Holden's Circulating Library of Windsor Locks, Conn., circulated its 650 volumes 750 times in 1876, deriving a total income therefrom of $50 [USBE *Public Libraries*]

Holton Circulating Library in Danvers, Mass., was established about 1836 and lasted five years [Shera]

Lyman Homiston's Circulating Library was in operation in Salem, Mass., in 1804 [Tapley]

R. Horton, see Franklin Library (Pawtucket, R.I.)

Houston (Tex.) Circulating Library and Reading

Room, was opened by Martin Kingsley Snell in 1844 and continued in business for about five years [Hatch]

Howe & Deforest's Circulating Library of New Haven, Conn., produced a 40-page catalogue of its collection in 1814 [Shera]

Benjamin R. Howland, see Robinson & Howland's Circulating Library

Hoyt's Circulating Library in Chester, Vt., held 500 volumes in 1876 [USBE *Public Libraries*]

Hunt, Sim & Co., see Champaign County Circulating Library

Hunter & Robinson's Circulating Library with 2,000 volumes was opened by James A. Hunter and Joseph Robinson of Baltimore in 1809 and was taken over by the latter a year later, by which time its collections had grown to some 5,000 volumes; it issued catalogues in both years [Silver's *Baltimore*, Shaw]

Lucy L. Hunter's Circulating Library in Baltimore continued William Munday's operation following his death in 1819; it issued a catalogue in 1882! [Silver's *Baltimore*]

Hurd's Circulating Library of Titusville, Pa., had some 1,100 volumes in 1876 [USBE *Public Libraries*]

Christian Jacob Hütter's Circulating Library in Lancaster, Pa., was opened in January 1800 and claimed to have 4,000 volumes six months later [Knauss]

Indian Queen Tavern Reading Room was an enterprise of J. Gadsby of Baltimore in 1818 [Silver's *Baltimore*]

Indianapolis Reading Room was proposed by bookseller T. J. Langdon in 1830; it would be "fitted up at his public house, opposite the Court House" [*Indianapolis State Gazette*, July 29, 1830]

Irving Circulating Library (New York), conducted by W. H. Attree, issued a catalogue in 1842 [*National Union Catalog*]

Irving Circulating Library (Washington, D.C.) possessed 1,100 volumes in 1876, the second year of its existence [USBE *Public Libraries*]

Irving's Reading Room was located at 178 North Third Street in Philadelphia in 1836 [*New Yorker*, June 11, 1836]

John M. Ives, see Essex Circulating Library (Salem, Mass.)

Jamaica Plain (Mass.) Circulating Library, which had been founded eight years earlier, reported a collection of 1,200 volumes in 1876 [USBE *Public Libraries*]

Thomas Johnson's Circulating Library was operating in Columbus, Ohio, in 1825 [Martin]

Johnson's Circulating Library was established in Laconia, N.H., in 1870 and contained 500 volumes six years later [USBE *Public Libraries*]

Miss Jordan's Circulating Library was opened in Lancaster, Pa., in 1821 and continued for about a quarter of a century [Ellis/Evans]

Charles Jourdan's Circulating Library was carrying on business in New Orleans in 1816 [McCutcheon]

Juvenile Circulating Library was operated by Mayhew & Baker along with their Central Circulating Library in Boston; it issued a catalogue in 1860.

Kelly's Circulating Library in Troy, Ohio, was founded in 1868; eight years later it claimed to own 585 volumes [USBE *Public Libraries*]

Kendrick's Circulating Library at 103 Main Street in Saco, Me., issued a catalogue of its holdings in the 1880s.

Kenyon's Circulating Library in Dwight, Ill., was only two years old in 1876 but was nonetheless already circulating its 800 volumes some 3,000 times annually [USBE *Public Libraries*]

Archibald Kerr's Circulating Library was in business in Washington, Pa., in 1832 [Crumrine]

Joseph B. Kidder, see Roxbury Circulating Library

Kimball & Ward's Punch House and Reading Room was maintained in St. Louis, Mo. in 1818 [*Missouri Gazette*, May 15, 1818]

O. C. King's Circulating Library was established in Woodstock, Vt., in 1835 [Shera]

Kirby's Circulating Library in Elkhart, Ind., contained 600 volumes in 1876 [USBE *Public Libraries*]

Emil Klauprecht's Circulating Library purveyed primarily German books to Cincinnatians in 1839 [Cazden]

Ladies Circulating Library (Boston) was located at 45½ Newbury Street in 1820; it issued a catalogue in 1829 [Silver's *Boston*]

Ladies' Circulating Library (Middlebury, Vt.) appears to have issued a catalogue [*National Union Catalog*]

Jacob Lahn, see German Circulating Library

George Lamb's Circulating Library opened in Savannah, Ga., in 1798 and continued in business for about a year [Moore]

Samuel Larkin's Circulating Library in Portsmouth, N.H., issued a catalogue of its holdings in 1796.

Lawrence & Co.'s Circulating Library in Red Wing, Minn., which was founded in 1874, was circulating its thousand volumes 9,000 times annually by 1876 [USBE *Public Libraries*]

B. G. Levi's Circulating Library in Cincinnati was located at 107 Main Street in 1835 [Sutton]

Frederick Leypoldt's Circulating Library and Reading Room was at the corner of Chestnut and Juniper in Philadelphia; in 1864 he closed it and sold its 6,000 volumes to the Mercantile Library [Growoll]

Librairie de la Famille in New Orleans appears to have been a profit-seeking venture; in 1876 its 25,000 volumes reportedly circulated 50,000 times [USBE *Public Libraries*]

Lindsley's Circulating Library in Boston advertised 3,000 volumes in 1876 and a growth rate of 300 volumes per year [USBE *Public Libraries*]

Liscom's Circulating Library in Boston was allegedly established in 1869; it reported holding 1,000 volumes seven years later with gross annual receipts totalling $600, of which $100 went for new books [USBE *Public Libraries*]

Edward Little & Co.'s Circulating Library, Newburyport, Mass., was bought from William Sawyer & Co., in 1809 [Shera]

John Lockwood's Circulating Library existed in Alexandria, Va., in 1792 [Noble]

John Lockwood's Circulating Library of more than 1,000 volumes in Suter's Tavern in Georgetown in 1792 may have been a branch of his Alexandria operation [Noble]

Lodi (N.J.) Circulating Library was established in 1846 and reported holding 2,500 volumes three decades later [USBE *Public Libraries*]

John Longhurst's Circulating Library was located on Court Street in Boston in 1811 [Silver's *Boston*]

A. K. Loring's Select Circulating Library, which was opened in Boston in 1859, contained about 10,000 volumes in 1876; it experimented for a time with house-to-house delivery and produced a catalogue in 1863 [Bolton, USBE *Public Libraries*]

Los Angeles Circulating Library existed in 1871 [Held]

Samuel Loudon's Circulating Library was opened at No. 5, Water Street, in New York City in 1773 and continued in business until at least 1785 [McKay]

Louisville (Ky.) Circulating Library issued a catalogue of some 1,225 titles in 1842.

Charles F. Lummis' Circulating Library was in operation between 1827 and 1832 in Lynn, Mass. [Shera]

Lynn (Mass.) Circulating Library opened in 1822 [Shera]

John M'Donald's Circulating Library was located on Fourth Street in Philadelphia between 1798 and the end of the century [Browns' *Philadelphia*]

John M'Donald's Circulating Library was purchased from Hugh Somerville of Washington, D.C. sometime after 1801 [Noble]

Joseph McIntire's Circulating Library in Pawtucket, R.I., was offered for sale in 1845 [Browns' *R.I.*]

Mack & Andrus' Circulating Library and Reading Room was maintained adjacent to their bookstore in Ithaca, N.Y., in 1825 and 1826 [*Ithaca Journal*, June 15, 1825; May 3, 1826]

Malone's Circulating Library in La Salle, Ill., was established in 1874; in 1876 its 450 books circulated 1,700 times, earning the proprietor $100 [USBE *Public Libraries*]

Manson's Circulating Library was opened in Paterson, N.J., in 1865; in 1876 its proprietor grossed $1,500 from circulating its 2,000 volumes 26,000 times [USBE *Public Libraries*]

Angier March, see Essex Circulating Library (Newburyport)

Silas Marchant's Circulating Library was maintained in 1832 in his lottery office in Pawtucket, R. I. [Browns' *R.I.*]

H. C. Marsh's Circulating Library was owned and operated by the postmaster of Muncie, Ind., from 1868 to 1875, at which time his books were purchased to become the nucleus of the new Muncie Public Library [Henry]

Marshall's Circulating Library in Rochester, N.Y., was in business between 1823 and 1825 [McKelvey]

William Martin, see Boston Circulating Library

Maryland Circulating Library was maintained by Nathaniel P. Bixley on the northwest corner of Charles and Conewago Streets in Baltimore from 1820 until it was absorbed into the Baltimore Athenaeum in 1824; it published a catalogue and at least two supplements listing its holdings [Silver's *Baltimore*]

Maspero's Reading Room was located upstairs in his coffee house in New Orleans in 1814 [Kaser's *Coffee House*]

Eaton Maxcy's Circulating Library appears to have been run in conjunction with his printing and publishing activities in Providence, R.I., in the late 1820s [Browns' *R.I.*]

Mayhew & Baker, see Central Circulating Library (Boston); Juvenile Circulating Library

S. W. Meech, see Franklin Circulating Library (St. Louis, Mo.)

John Mein's Circulating Library operated in Boston for a short time following its establishment in 1765 [Bolton]

Mendenhall's Circulating Library was established in Cincinnati in 1854; in 1876 it contained some 6,000 volumes and was accessioning 300 additional volumes annually [USBE *Public Libraries*]

Merrell & Hastings' Circulating Library which was "kept at their book store, No.40, Genesee Street" in Utica, N.Y., issued a 12-page catalogue of its collections in 1823 [Shoemaker]

Merrill's Circulating Library in Boston reported holdings totalling 4,000 volumes in 1876 [USBE *Public Libraries*]

Merrimac Circulating Library, 2 Middle Street in Newburyport, Mass., was established in 1807 by Webb & Kettell and was run by W. & J. Gilman, printers, between 1815 and 1839 [Shera]

Charles Metcalf, see Boston Circulating Library

P. Michael's Circulating Library was located in Ohio, Ill. [Sharp]

Miller & Hutchens' Circulating Library was taken over from Robinson & Howland of Providence in 1816 [Browns' *R.I.*]

John Milligan, see Union Circulating Library (Georgetown, D.C.)

John Milliquet's Circulating Library was maintained in his bookstore at 1 Cambridge Street, Boston, from 1803 to 1805 [Silver's *Boston*]

Minerva Circulating Library (New York) was located at 106 Chatham Street in 1811 and 263 Broadway nine years later [McKay]

Minerva Circulating Library (Providence, R.I.) was conducted by "Mrs. Remington" at her female academy in Broad Street in 1809 [Browns' *R.I.*]

Missouri Advocate Reading Room was announced in St. Louis in 1826 [McDermott]

Missouri Gazette Reading Room appears to have been maintained by Joseph Charless in St. Louis in 1810 [Kaser's *Charless*]

Moniteur Circulating Library in New Orleans was operating in 1811 [McCutcheon]

Charles Morgan's Circulating Library was established in Charleston, S.C., in 1782 [Moore]

L. & M. Morse's Circulating Library in Rochester, N.Y., was established in 1824 [McKelvey]

Morse & Sons Circulating Library in Haverhill, Mass., was established in 1869 and reportedly held some 2,000 volumes seven years later [USBE *Public Libraries*]

William Munday, see Baltimore Circulating Library

Edward Murden, see Museum Circulating Library

William Murphy's Circulating Library, "at Yorick's Head in Market Street," Baltimore, was founded in 1784 and contained 2,000 volumes two years later when it was sold to Hugh Barkley [Moore, Evans, Reichmann]

Museum Circulating Library was operated by Edward Murden at No. 4 Chamber Street near Chatham in New York City; a copy of its 34-page catalogue of its collection produced in 1822 is preserved in the New York Public Library.

Napa Circulating Library was operated by a druggist in this California community before 1870 [Held]

Melitiah Nash's Circulating Library at 79 Beekman Street in New York published a catalogue of its holding in 1803.

Mrs. Christina Neale, see Union Circulating Library (Philadelphia)

Nevada City (Cal.) Reading Room, located in the back room of a general store, supplied newspapers left unclaimed at the Sacramento post office [Wood]

New Circulating Library (Boston) at 82 Newbury Street, issued a catalogue in 1804.

New Circulating Library (Newport, R.I.) located at 93 Thames Street produced a catalogue of its collection in 1808 [Shaw]

New Circulating Library (Philadelphia) was opened by Lewis Nicola in 1767; in 1769 he changed its name to the General Circulating Library [Lamberton, Bridenbaugh's *Rebels*, Silver's *Philadelphia*]

New London (Conn.) Circulating Library was flourishing in 1793 [Shera]

Newburyport Circulating Library in Massachusetts was kept by Charles Whipple at No.4 State Street; it issued a catalogue in 1816.

Lewis Nicola, see New Circulating Library (Philadelphia); General Circulating Library

Nimmo's Circulating Library in Washington, D.C., which was opened in 1867, possessed some 3,000 volumes nine years later and was grossing $1,800 annually [USBE *Public Libraries*]

Garret Noel's Circulating Library, the first in New

York City, was opened in 1763 but continued in business only a short time [Keep]

Norfolk Circulating Library was opened in 1865 in Norfolk, Conn.; it held 348 volumes in 1876 [USBE *Public Libraries*]

Norton's Circulating Library of Scranton, Pa., contained 1,000 volumes in 1876 [USBE *Public Libraries*]

Louis Oldenburg, see Washington Hall Reading Room

Benjamin Olds' Circulating Library was being operated out of his bookstore in Newark, N.J., "within a few years" after 1819 [Sabine]

Joseph Osborn's Circulating Library in New York City was taken over from Hocquet Caritat in 1804 and remained in operation at least three years [McKay, "Literary Intelligence"]

George Osburne's Circulating Library was being maintained in his Newburyport, Mass., bookstore, as early as 1794 [Shera]

Painesville (Ohio) Circulating Library was operated by George E. H. Day in conjunction with his bookstore in 1831-1833, and by W. Whittaker as an adjunct to his bookbindery in 1841 [Stiffler]

G. Painter's Reading Room in New York City was proposed in 1798 [Thompson]

Palmer & Trumbull's Library in Stonington, Conn., was established in 1872; four years later it contained 625 volumes, was recording 5,000 loans per year, and was grossing $225 annually, all of which was spent for books [USBE *Public Libraries*]

Samuel H. Parker, see Union Circulating Library (Boston)

Parker's Circulating Library of Lewiston, Me., lent out its 870 books a total of 10,000 times in 1876, earning therefrom $500 [USBE *Public Libraries*]

Parkhurst & Brother, see Franklin Circulating Library (Providence); Waverly Circulating Library

H. Parmelee Library Company was established in Des Moines in 1882 but removed early to Chicago and developed a chain of circulating libraries; it went bankrupt in 1902 [Sharp]

Pawtucket Reading Room was being conducted in 1832 by Stephen G. Benedict [Browns' *R.I.*]

Elizabeth Peabody, see Foreign Library

Pearson & Little, see Washington Circulating Library (Washington, Me.)

Charles Peirce's Circulating Library, operating out of his Brick Bookstore in Portsmouth, N.H., issued a catalogue of its holdings in 1806.

William Pelham's Circulating Library was opened in 1796 at No.59, Cornhill, in Boston and was transferred to William Blagrove eight years later; it published catalogues in 1801 and 1804 [Silver's *Boston*, Bolton; see also Union Circulating Library (Philadelphia)]

Elias Penniman, Jr., Scc Boston Circulating Library

Pentagon Circulating Library of Suncook, N.H., was established in 1875 and was still in business sixteen years later [USBE *Report*, N.H. State Librarian's *Report* 1891]

Peoria (Ill.) Circulating Library was being maintained in the 1850s by Edward J. Cowell [Eaton]

Daniel Perrin's Circulating Library was founded in Providence, R.I., in 1820 by George Dana and taken over in 1849 by Perrin; in 1854 its 5,000 volumes circulated 20,000 times to 2,500 patrons resulting in a gross annual income of $1,300. By 1876 the collection had grown to 6,000 volumes [Browns' *R.I.* Rhees, USBE *Public Libraries*]

Philadelphia Circulating Library issued a catalogue in 1824 [Shoemaker]

John Phillips' Circulating Library was located in his bookstore at 22-24 South Third in Philadelphia from 1801 to 1811 when he disposed of it to Francis and Ann Shallus [Browns' *Philadelphia*, Mease]

Phoenix Circulating Library, Newburyport, Mass., was established in 1837 by John Gray, Jr., and sold five years later to A. A. Call [Shera]

Arthur E. Pierce's Reading Room and Circulating Library in Denver, Colo., was operating as early as 1850 and was sold in 1860 to Woolworth & Moffat [Poste]

John K. Pitman's Circulating Library of 1,400 volumes was offered for sale at his bookstore in Providence, R.I., in 1812 [Browns' *R.I.*]

Pittsburgh Reading Room was operating in 1833 [Anderson]

Planters' Banner Reading Room in Franklin, La., was opened in 1847 by Robert Wilson and kept open for three years [Patrick]

Thomas Porter's Circulating Library was operated in conjunction with his bookstore in Salem, Mass., in 1812 [Tapley]

Porter & Ide's Circulating Library of Warren, Ohio, advertised its willingness to accept country produce in exchange for subscription in 1842 [Stiffler]

Portsmouth (N.H.) Circulating Library was owned by Shores, Foster & Co.; a copy of its 64-page catalogue published in 1866 is preserved in the New York Public Library.

Post & Co.'s Circulating Library in Cincinnati operated at three different locations between 1847 and midcentury [Sutton]

Post Meridian Reading Room was maintained in 1828 by proprietor H. P. Bradbury in his Post Meridian tavern in St. Louis; he sold it the following year [McDermott]

Pottstown Circulating Library in Pennsylvania had some 750 volumes in 1876, from which it derived income amounting to $100 per year [USBE *Public Libraries*]

Zachariah Poulson's Circulating Library was maintained in connection with his printing and publishing business in Philadelphia through the turn of the eighteenth century [Browns' *Philadelphia*]

Pratt & Nichols' Circulating Library was opened in 1837 in Rochester, N.Y. [McKelvey]

John Prentiss' Circulating Library was established in his bookstore and printing office in Keene, N.H., in 1805 [Shera]

William Prentiss' Reading Room was established in Washington, D.C., in 1815 but failed for want of subscribers [Noble]

William Prichard's Circulating Library on Market

Street in Philadelphia, was in operation at least as early as 1783, when it issued a catalogue, until 1788 [Browns' *Philadelphia*, Evans]

Providence Cheapside Circulating Library in Rhode Island was owned by Nathaniel Dearborn who sold it to Wanton & Rathbone in 1810 [Browns' *R.I.*]

Putnam Circulating Library, founded in Elizabeth, N.J., in 1875, reported holding 500 volumes a year later [USBE *Public Libraries*]

Joseph Rathell's Circulating Library in Baltimore, Md., was proposed in 1773, but appears never to have opened [Moore]

E. Rawson's Circulating Library, located on the northwest corner of Walnut and Second Streets in Philadelphia, was offered for sale in 1813 [Browns' *Philadelphia*]

Reading and News Room was located at 129 Bowery in New York City in 1814 [McKay]

Reading Room (Wadsworth, Ohio) was maintained in a Main Street millinery shop following 1822 [Stiffler]

Thomas Reddish, see Sun Circulating Library

Lydia Reed's Circulating Library was located in Cambridge, Massachusetts in 1825 [Silver's *Boston*]

Mrs. Remington, see Minerva Circulating Library (Providence)

Allen Reynolds' Circulating Library was purchased from John B. Walker of Woonsocket, R. I., in 1838 [Browns' *R.I.*]

Rhees Circulating Library of Mount Holly, N.J., reported earning $130 from its 600-volume collection in 1876 [USBE *Public Libraries*]

Anstis E. Richardson's Circulating Library, which was located three doors west of the Newport, R.I. *Mercury* in 1817, appears still to have been in operation two score years later [Browns' *R.I.*]

Richland Library, in existence in 1857 in Quakerstown, Pa., appears to have been a commercial enterprise [Rhees]

William Rind's Circulating Library, the first attempted in the American colonies, was opened in Annapolis, Md., in 1763 but soon failed for want of subscribers [Wheeler]

J. Roach & Co.'s Circulating Library at 38 Market

Street in Baltimore in 1820 was still in business five years later; Shaw and Shoemaker's attribution of its catalogue to the year 1807 appears to be incorrect [Silver's *Baltimore*]

Joseph Robinson's Circulating Library was taken over from Hunter & Robinson of Baltimore in 1810, and it published regular catalogues of its holdings and accessions for about ten years thereafter; in 1839 it contained some 17,000 volumes, but it appears to have been disbanded soon thereafter [Silver's *Baltimore*, Moore]

Martin Robinson's Circulating Library of Providence, R.I., issued catalogues in 1823, 1825, 1827, and again in 1829 [See also Robinson & Beckwith's Circulating Library; Robinson & Howland's Circulating Library]

Solon Robinson's Circulating Library was founded in his Madison, Ind., auction rooms in 1834 [Keller]

Robinson & Beckwith's Circulating Library, Providence, R.I., was run by Martin Robinson and A. S. Beckwith until the former took over its sole proprietorship in 1826 [Browns' *R.I.*; see also Robinson & Howland's Circulating Library; Martin Robinson's Circulating Library]

Robinson & Howland's Circulating Library and Reading Room of Providence, R.I., was maintained in connection with their bookstore from 1813 forward for several years [Browns' *R.I.*; See also Martin Robinson's Circulating Library; Robinson & Beckwith's Circulating Library]

P[ierre?] Roche's Circulating Library was opened at No.4, South Gay Street in Baltimore in 1804 [Silver's *Baltimore*]

Widow Roche's Circulating Library was maintained in conjunction with her stationery store in New Orleans following 1811 [McCutcheon]

Rochester (N.Y.) Telegraph Reading Room received a $20 donation in 1826 from J. Wadsworth of Geneseo, N.Y. [Hamilton]

Rodger's Arctic Library, at Libbysville near Teller in Alaska contained 50 volumes in 1867 [Stewart]

Edwin Rogers' Circulating Library, at his store at Main and Eagle Streets in North Adams, Mass., advertised 800 volumes in 1844 [Shera]

Roman Catholic Library was maintained by Bernard

Dornin on Baltimore and Saratoga Streets between 1810 and 1816 [Silver's *Baltimore*]

Roxbury Circulating Library, was operated by Joseph B. Kidder of Boston from 1822 to 1825 [Silver's *Boston*]

H. H. Russell's Circulating Library was maintained in conjunction with his periodical dealership in the Post Office building of Pawtucket, R.I., between 1863 and 1865 [Browns' *R.I.*]

G. L. Ryder's Circulating Library of Massillon, Ohio, was founded in 1870 and owned some 800 volumes six years later [USBE *Public Libraries*]

Saco (Me.) Circulating Library, kept by A. E. Small, issued a catalogue of its collections in 1834.

St. John's Circulating Library in St. Louis, Mo., founded in 1872, held 600 volumes four years later [USBE *Public Libraries*]

St. Louis Circulating Library was located at 76 Chestnut Street in 1845 [Kaser's *St. Louis*]

St. Louis Reading Room was in existence in 1831 [McDermott]

St. Peter's Theological Library, see Theological Library (Baltimore, Md.)

San Carlos Circulating Library was in operation in this California town in 1864 [Held]

San Rafael Circulating Library in California was in business in 1871 [Held]

Sandwich (Mass.) Circulating Library was founded in 1864 and held 1,200 volumes twelve years later [USBE *Public Libraries*]

Sanford & Co.'s Circulating Library was opened in Cleveland, Ohio, in 1841 [Stiffler, Martin]

Santa Barbara Library, containing some 400 volumes, was founded by a California school teacher in 1870 and was operated in a jewelry store [Held]

Saratoga Springs (N.Y.) Reading Room advertised in 1819 that it could provide "most of the important daily, semi-weekly, and weekly newspapers of our country," and intended to add a circulating library later [Hamilton]

Ezra Sargeant's Reading Room was maintained in his

bookstore at 86 Broadway in New York City in 1809 and 1810 [McKay]

William Sawyer & Co.'s Circulating Library of Newburyport, Mass., was purchased from E. Stedman in 1807 and sold two years later to Edward Little & Co. [Shera]

Louis Schwarz's Circulating Library, opened in New Orleans in 1857 with 20,000 volumes, carried a large stock of German titles [Cazden]

T. Scott's Reading Room and Circulating Library was operated in conjunction with his land office in Rochester, N.Y. [McKelvey]

Sentinel Circulating Library of Eastport, Me., which was established in 1866, contained 800 volumes a decade later [USBE *Public Libraries*]

Shakspeare Circulating Library was maintained in Boston by Charles Callender from 1815 to his death about 1840 and thereafter by his family for some fifteen years; it produced catalogues of its holdings in 1815, 1819, and 1820 [Silver's *Boston*, Bolton]

Ann Shallus' Circulating Library was listed in the New Orleans city directory for 1822.

Shallus' Circulating Library was acquired from John Phillips in 1811 by Francis and Ann Shallus and was operated by them for a decade thereafter at several locations on Third Street in Philadelphia [Browns' *Philadelphia*]

Shores, Foster & Co., see Portsmouth (N.H.) Circulating Library

Siebert's Circulating Library of Renovo, Pa., reported holding 304 volumes in 1876 [USBE *Public Libraries*]

George Sinclair's Circulating Library was operated in connection with his bookbindery at 207 Water Street in New York in 1805 and 1806 [McKay]

H. C. Sleight's Circulating Library of Jamaica, N.Y., issued a catalogue of its collections in 1824 [Shoemaker]

A. E. Small, see Saco (Me.) Circulating Library

Martin Kingsley Snell, see Houston (Tex.) Circulating Library

Daniel Snyder's Circulating Library was in operation in Philadelphia in 1822 [MacFarlane]

Alexander Somerville's Circulating Library opened at 114 Maiden Lane in New York City in 1800 but was sold to William Barlas before the year was out [Raddin's *Hocquet Caritat*]

Hugh Somerville's Circulating Library, which he had established in his store in Washington, D.C., in 1801, was sold later to John M'Donald [Noble]

South End Circulating Library of Worcester, Mass., was getting an annual 4,000 circulations from its collection of 300 volumes in 1876 [USBE *Public Libraries*]

Sparta (Ill.) Circulating Library was three years old in 1876, when it reported that its 594 volumes had been lent out 745 times for a gross earning of $95 [USBE *Public Libraries*]

Mary Sprague's Circulating Library was situated in her millinery shop, 9 Milk Street in Boston, from 1802 to 1806 [Silver's *Boston*]

Staughton Circulating Library in Massachusetts circulated its 700 volumes 2,500 times in 1876 for a gross income of $300 [USBE *Public Libraries*]

Ebenezer Stedman's Circulating Library in Newburyport, Mass., was acquired from Edmund Blunt in 1803 and sold to William Sawyer & Co. four years later [Shera]

Sterling & Mosher's Circulating Library was founded in Watertown, N.Y., in 1867; nine years later it claimed to have 1,800 volumes [USBE *Public Libraries*]

Erastus Sterry, see Dearth & Sterry's Circulating Library

Stevens' Circulating Library in Saratoga Springs, N.Y., was opened in 1874; in 1876 it reported holding 550 volumes and an annual circulation of 200 [USBE *Public Libraries*]

Stevens & Co.'s Circulating Library in Lewiston, Me., recorded a circulation of 15,000 in 1876 from its collection of a thousand volumes, grossing an income of $500; the library was then three years old [USBE *Public Libraries*]

Henry J. Stevenson's Circulating Library was located on Marlborough Street in Boston between 1806 and 1809 [Silver's *Boston*]

Stockton Library in Pottsville, Pa., appears to have been a commercial venture; founded in 1860, it reported holding 4,000 volumes sixteen years later, which circulated 13,500 times in 1876 producing income amounting to $374 [USBE *Public Libraries*]

Elihu Stout's Reading Room was maintained in his printing office in Vincennes, Ind., following 1814 [Dunn's *Libraries*]

A. S. & G. M. Streeter's Circulating Library and lottery office in Woonsocket Falls, R.I., issued a catalogue in 1833; it was sold to E. M. and A. C. Hawes the following year [Browns' *R.I.*]

Sun Circulating Library, operated by bookseller Thomas Reddish of Cincinnati, contained 2,000 volumes in 1819; in 1828 it was located in Third Street near the Post Office [Sutton, Martin]

Tappan's Circulating Library of Portsmouth, N.H., published a catalogue listing its holdings in 1809.

B. Taylor, see Albion Library

Terrasse's Coffee House Reading Room in Lexington, Ky., in 1807 kept files of forty-two newspapers from around the nation [Cuming]

Theological Circulating Library, at 95 Court Street in Boston, was opened in 1814 by Joseph T. Buckingham, printer and editor [Silver's *Boston*]

Theological Library (Baltimore, Md.) was opened at 56 South Charles Street in 1812 by John Creery, who then offered it for sale in 1815 [Silver's *Baltimore*]

Charles Thomas' Circulating Library was conducting business in New Orleans in 1816 [McCutcheon]

Joshua Thomas' Circulating Library, "opposite the Treasurer's Office" in Boston in 1793, sought "the patronage of the LADIES of *Boston*" [*Boston Independent Chronicle*, June 27, 1793]

S. T. Thurber's Circulating Library in Providence, R.I., comprised 4,000 volumes when it was offered for sale by Adams Foster in 1836 [Browns' *R.I.*]

Thwing's Circulating Library in Great Falls, N.H. was established in 1872 and continued for at least twenty years; its 500-volume collection earned $300 for the proprietors in 1876 [USBE *Public Libraries*, USBE *Report*, N.H. State Librarian's *Report* 1891]

John G. Tilton, see Washington Circulating Library (Newburyport, Mass.)

Amos Trask, Jr., see Franklin Circulating Library (Danvers, Mass.)

John Trumbull's Circulating Library of Norwich, Conn., published a catalogue of its holdings in 1796 [Sills]

Underwood Library of Russellville, Ky., which existed in 1857, appears to have been a commercial enterprise [Rhees]

Union Circulating Library (Boston), was taken over by William Blagrove in 1805 and merged with Pelham's Circulating Library which he had purchased a year earlier; it was relinquished in 1811 to Samuel Parker, and its collections were dispersed in 1833; it published catalogues in 1806, 1810, 1815, and 1820 [Silver's *Boston*, Bolton]

Union Circulating Library (Georgetown, D.C.) was kept by John Milligan in his bookstore from 1813 to 1820, when he sold it to Davis & Force [Noble]

Union Circulating Library (Philadelphia) was owned by William Pelham until 1814 when he sold it to Christina Neale, who operated it in her bookstore on Chestnut adjacent to the New Theatre; a catalogue of its holdings was published in 1824 [Browns' *Philadelphia*]

Union Library (Phenix, R.I.) was conducted in 1860-61, along with his reading and picture rooms, at no.4 upstairs in Spencer's Building by W. P. Andrew [Browns' *R.I.*]

Universal Circulating Library, advertised by Robert Bell of Philadelphia in 1774, issued a catalogue four years later [Lamberton, Bridenbaugh's *Rebels*, Evans]

E. Vallette & Co.'s Circulating Library in Baltimore was to have held 2,500 volumes in 1793, according to its proposal [Moore]

Aarondt Van Hook's Reading Room on Water Street in New York City contained a small "standing library" in 1797 [Raddin's *Hocquet Caritat*]

Volanco (Cal.) Circulating Library rented books at 10 Cents each in the 1850s [Wood]

S. M. Vose's Circulating Library in Providence, R.I., was situated at 186 Westminster in 1857 [Browns' *R.I.*]

John B. Walker's Circulating Library in Woonsocket, R.I., was sold to Allen Reynolds in 1838 [Browns' *R.I.*]

T. O. Walker's Circulating Library in Boston was reportedly strong in French novels in the early 1840s [Shera]

Wanton & Rathbone's Circulating Library in Newport, R.I., was purchased from Nathaniel Dearborn of Providence in 1810 and sold to James Hammond of Newport in 1811 [Browns' *R.I.*, Shera]

H. G. O. Washburn's Circulating Library in Belfast, Me., was founded in 1844 [Shera]

Washington Circulating Library (Boston) in Newbury Street, issued a catalogue in 1817.

Washington Circulating Library (Newburyport, Mass.) was established in 1840 by John G. Tilton; except for a closure from 1846 to 1851, it remained in business until the Newburyport Public Library opened in 1855 [Shera]

Washington Circulating Library (Washington, D.C.) was bought by Davis & Force from Joseph Milligan of Georgetown in 1820; it issued three catalogues in the next two years, the last of which listed 3,600 volumes [Noble]

Washington Circulating Library (Washington, Me.) located in "the bookstore of Pearson & Little," issued a catalogue of its holdings in 1829.

Washington Hall Reading Room in the Washington Hall hotel in St. Louis was announced in 1831 by proprietor Louis Oldenburg [McDermott]

Washington Library, at 281 Walnut Street in Philadelphia in 1829, appears to have been a commercial lending library [Royall]

Waterville Circulating Library, established in 1826 and operated for two years by William Hastings, saw its 700 volumes catalogued in the *Waterville (Me.) Intelligencer*, October 19, 26; November 2, 9, 1826 [Shera]

Waverly Circulating Library (Providence, R.I.) was an enterprise of Parkhurst & Brother, music and bookdealers, at 100 Westminster in 1849 [Browns' *R.I.*]

Waverly Circulating Library (Waverly, Me.) situated at No. 8, Mussey's Row Middle Street, issued a catalogue in 1828 enumerating its holdings [Shoemaker]

Webb & Kettell, see Merrimac Circulating Library

George Weller's Circulating Library of Newark, N.J., was sold in 1814 [Sabine]

West Side Library, 239 W. Madison Street in Chicago, was opened in 1869 by Emerson & Stott of the Western News Co.; it held 6,000 volumes in 1876 and later operated several branches throughout the city [Spencer, USBE *Public Libraries*]

Westermann's Circulating Library was located at 290 Broadway in New York in the second half of the nineteenth century; it specialized in supplying books in the German language [Hoffman]

Weston's Pioneer Library, founded in Boston in 1865, had 850 volumes a decade later; it reported circulating 900 books per year and grossing $450 annually, of which it spent $250 for books [USBE *Public Libraries*]

Whig Reading Room in Richmond, Ind., was "well supplied with valuable documents and papers" and available to subscribers in 1838 [*Richmond (Ind.) Palladium,* Feb. 3, 1838]

Charles Whipple, see Newburyport Circulating Library

Ezra D. Whitaker's Circulating Library was established in North Adams, Mass., in 1830 [Shera]

Whitcomb & Cook, see Fitchburg Circulating Library

Whitinsville (Mass.) Circulating Library was established in 1857 [Rhees]

W. Whittaker, See Painesville (Ohio) Circulating Library

Whittemore's Circulating Library of Kansas City, Mo., contained a thousand books in 1876 [USBE *Public Libraries*]

T. Whybrew's Circulating Library was operated in Newark, N.J., from 1823 to 1825 [Sabine]

John Wilcocks' Circulating Library was conducted in his bookselling and bookbinding establishment in Providence, R.I., between 1850 and 1865 [Browns' *R.I.*]

W. S. Wilder, see Fitchburg Circulating Library

William R. Wilder's Circulating Library in Newport, R.I., opened in 1798 with a collection of some 1,500 volumes and continued in business for a decade [Browns' *R.I.*]

J. Wilkins' Circulating Library was established in Astor, Wisc., in 1838 [Saucerman]

Robert Williams' Circulating Library was being run from his newsstand in Harrisville, R.I., in 1861 [Browns' *R.I.*]

John D. Wilson, Jr.'s, Circulating Library served a public in Salem, Mass., in 1819-21 [Shera]

Robert Wilson, see *Planters' Banner* Reading Room

Wilson's Circulating Library was founded in Philadelphia with some 3,000 volumes in 1875; within a decade it had grown to 22,000 volumes and was operating branches elsewhere in Pennsylvania and in New Jersey [Scharf & Westcott]

Winsor's Circulating Library of 4,700 volumes in Providence, R.I., circulated 20,000 books to 2,000 patrons in 1857, grossing $1,340; it had been established nine years earlier [Rhees]

George Wood's Circulating Library in Charleston, S.C., was proposed in 1763 and continued in business for four years [Moore]

William E. Woodruff's Circulating Library in Little Rock, Ark., was founded in 1843 and suffered losses during the Civil War twenty years later [Hutchins]

R. Jones Woodward, see City Circulating Library (St. Louis, Mo.)

Woolworth & Colt's Circulating Library in St. Joseph, Mo., owned 1,500 volumes in 1876 [USBE *Public Libraries*]

Worrell's Circulating Library of Red Bank, N.J., was founded in 1870; in 1876 it contained some 600 volumes whence it grossed $300 [USBE *Public Libraries*]

Wyoming (Ill.) Circulating Library contained 120 volumes in 1887 [Sharp]

Yallop's Circulating Library was opened in Milwaukee in 1851 and contained 800 volumes six years later [Rhees]

William Yearnshaw's Circulating Library was kept in his intelligence office in "the next Building north of Rathburn's Block" in Woonsocket, R.I., in 1844 [Browns' *R.I.*]

Circulating Library Catalogues Examined in the
Course of this Study and Analyzed in Appendix II.

Aikman's (William) Circulating Library, Annapolis, Md.
   [Catalogue. Annapolis: n.p., 1773?] 67 p. (Maryland
   Historical Society)
American Circulating Library Company, Hillsdale, Mich.
   Catalogue of Books and Authors. Hillsdale, Mich.:
   n.p., 1886. 24 p. (Library of Congress)
Annapolis Circulating Library, Annapolis, Md. *Catalogue*
   of the . . . . Annapolis: Frederick & Samuel Green
   [1783] [49 p.] (Maryland Historical Society)
Baltimore Circulating Library, Baltimore, Md. *Catalogue*
   of the . . . , Kept by William Munday . . . . Baltimore:
   John W. Butler, 1807. 112 p. (Maryland Historical
   Society)
Baltimore Circulating Library, Baltimore, Md. *First Sup-*
   plement to the Catalogue of the . . . , Kept by William
   Munday. [Baltimore]: n.p., 1809. 24 p. (Maryland His-
   torical Society)
Baltimore Circulating Library, Baltimore, Md. *Catalogue*
   of the . . . , Kept by William Munday . . . . Baltimore:
   W. Warner, 1812. 43 p. (Maryland Historical Society)
Baltimore Circulating Library, Baltimore, Md. *First Sup-*
   plement to the Catalogue of the . . . , Kept by William
   Munday. Baltimore: William Warner, 1813. 8 p.
   (Maryland Historical Society)
Baltimore Circulating Library, Baltimore, Md. *Second Sup-*
   plement to the Catalogue of the . . . , Kept by William
   Munday. Baltimore: William Warner, 1814. 21 [i.e.31]
   p. (Maryland Historical Society)
Baltimore Circulating Library, Baltimore, Md. *Catalogue*
   of the . . . , Mrs. Lucy L. Hunter, Prop. . . . . [Balti-
   more]: n.p., 1882. 56 p. (Maryland Historical Society)
Berrian's (Samuel) Circulating Library, New York. *Cata-*

logue of . . . . New York: G. & R. Waite, 1803. 91 p.
(New York Public Library)

Blake, William P. *Catalogue of Books, for Sale or Circulation* . . . . Boston: William Blake, 1793. 47 p. (Evans 25206)

Blake, William P. *Catalogue of Books, for Sale or Circulation* . . . . Boston: William P. Blake, 1796. 53 p. (New York Public Library)

Blake, William P. and Blake, Lemuel. *Catalogue of Books for Sale or Circulation* . . . . Boston: William P. & Lemuel Blake, 1798. 59 p. (Evans 33428)

Blake's (W. P. & L.) Circulating Library, Boston. *Catalogue of* . . . . Boston: William P. and Lemuel Blake, 1800. 48 p. (Boston Athenaeum)

Blake (William P.) & Co.'s Circulating Library, New York. *Catalogue of Books* . . . . New York: W. P. Blake & Co., 1818. 55 p. (New York Public Library)

Boylston Circulating-Library, Boston. *Catalogue of the* . . . . Boston: David Francis, 1837. 83 p. (Boston Public Library)

Cambridge Circulating Library, Cambridge, Mass. *Catalogue of the* . . . [Cambridge]: Sever and Francis, 1861. 35 p. (Boston Public Library)

Campbell's Circulating Library, Boston. *Catalogue of* . . . . Boston: James Campbell, 1870. 47 p. (Boston Public Library)

Caritat's (Hocquet) Circulating Library, New York. *The Feast of Reason and the Flow of Soul. A New Explanatory Catalogue of* . . . . New York: M. L. & W. A. Davis, 1799. 215 p. (New York Public Library)

Caritat's (Hocquet) Circulating Library, New York. *Explanatory Catalogue of* . . . . New York: G. & R. Waite [1804] 322 p. (New York Public Library)

Charter's (George) Circulating Library, New York. *Catalogue of Books in* . . . . New York: Van Winkle, Wiley & Co., 1817. 84, 16 p. (American Antiquarian Society)

Coleman and Chisholm's Circulating Library, Portland, Me. *Catalogue of* . . . . [Portland, Me.: n.p., 1837?] 25 p. (Maine Historical Society)

Coleman's (S.) Public Library, Portland, Me. *Catalogue of the* . . . . [Kept by S. Coleman. Portland, Me.: n.p., 1831] 14 p. (Maine Historical Society)

Coleman's (S.) Public Library, Portland, Me. *Catalogue of* . . . . Portland: n.p., [1834] 48 p. (Maine Historical Society)

Cushing and Appleton, Salem, Mass. *Catalogue of Books for Sale or Circulation, by* . . . . Salem, Mass.: Thomas C. Cushing, 1818. 108 p. (American Antiquarian Society)

Cushing's (Henry) Circulating Library, Providence, R.I. *Catalogue of* . . . . Providence: B. Wheeler, 1800. 39 p. (Rhode Island Historical Society)

Dabney, John. *Catalogue of Books, for Sale or Circulation* . . . . [Salem]: J. Dabney, 1791. 33 p. (Evans 23304)

Dabney, John. *Catalogue of Books, for Sale or Circulation* . . . . [Salem?]: n.p., 1801. 50 p. (Massachusetts Historical Society)

Dabney, John. *Additional Catalogue of Books, for Sale or Circulation* . . . . Newburyport, Mass.: Osborne, 1794. 34 p. (Evans 26840)

Dietrick's (Jacob D.) Circulating Library, Hagerstown, Md. *Catalogue of* . . . . Hagers-town, Md.: John Gruber, 1801. 98 p. (Washington County, Md., Public Library)

Ellis' Circulating Library, New Orleans, La. *Sixth Annual Catalogue* . . . . New Orleans: G. Ellis & brother, 1874. 66 p. (Library of Congress)

Essex Circulating Library, Salem, Mass. *A Supplementary Catalogue of the* . . . *, Kept by Cushing and Appleton* . . . . Salem: John D. Cushing, 1820. 12 p. (American Antiquarian Society)

Essex Circulating Library, Salem, Mass. *Catalogue of the* . . . *, Kept by John M. Ives* . . . . Salem: John D. Cushing and Brothers, 1822. 83 p. (Detroit Public Library)

Essex Circulating Library, Salem, Mass. *Catalogue of the* . . . . Salem: Andrews & Foote, 1826. 83 p. (Library Company of Philadelphia)

Foreign Library, Boston. *Catalogue of the* . . . . Boston:

S. N. Dickinson, 1840. 12 p. (Boston Public Library)

Foster, Drown & Company, Providence, R.I. [Catalogue] In Providence, R.I. *U.S. Chronicle*, June 11, 1789, 4: 2-3.

Franklin Circulating Library, Boston. *Catalogue of the . . . .* Boston: Sylvester T. Goss, 1820. 62 p. (Harvard University Library)

Franklin Circulating Library, Danvers, Mass. *Catalogue of the . . . .* Salem, Mass.: n.p., 1834. 23 p. (Massachusetts Historical Society)

Goodrich (A. T.) and Company's Circulating Library and Bookstore, New York. [Catalogue] New York: A. T. Goodrich, 1818. 118 p. (New York Public Library)

Guild, Benjamin. *Addition to a Catalogue of a Large Assortment of Books . . . to be Let or Sold . . . .* Boston: n.p. [1791?] 16 p. (Evans 45266)

Guild's (Benjamin) Circulating Library, Boston. *Select Catalogue of . . . .* Boston: Freeman, 1788. 20 p. (Harvard University Library)

Guild's (Benjamin) Circulating Library, Boston. *New Select Catalogue of . . . .* Boston: n.p., 1789. 36 p. (Evans 21868)

Harwood's (John) Circulating Library, Philadelphia. *Catalogue of . . . .* Philadelphia: William Duane, 1803. 120 p. (American Antiquarian Society)

Kendrick's Circulating Library, Saco, Me. *Catalogue of . . . .* Biddeford, Me.: *Union & Journal* Print. [188-?] 24 p. (Maine Historical Society)

Ladies' Circulating Library, Boston. *Catalogue of the . . . .* Boston: Putnam & Hunt, 1829. 66 p. (Harvard University Library)

Loring's (Aaron K.) Select Library, Boston. *Catalogue of . . . .* Boston: n.p. [1860] 20 p. (Boston Public Library)

Louisville Circulating Library, Louisville, Ky. *Catalogue of Books in the . . . .* Louisville: W. N. Haldeman, 1842. 13 p. (Indiana University Library)

Martin's (William) Circulating Library, Boston. *Catalogue of . . . .* [Boston]: Edmund Freeman, 1786. 16 p. (John Carter Brown Library)

Maryland Circulating Library, Baltimore, Md. *Catalogue of the Books Belonging to the* . . . . Baltimore: Frederick G. Shaeffer [1820?] 119 p. (Maryland Historical Society)

Maryland Circulating Library, Baltimore, Md. *Supplement to the Catalogue of Books, &c. Belonging to the* . . . . Baltimore: n.p. [1820?] 20 p. (Maryland Historical Society)

Maryland Circulating Library, Baltimore, Md. *No. 2 Supplement to the Catalogue of Books, &c* . . . . Baltimore: n.p., 1822. 34 p. (Maryland Historical Society)

Mayhew & Baker's Central Circulating Library, Boston. *Catalogue of* . . . . Boston: Mayhew & Baker, 1860. 30 p. (Boston Public Library)

Mayhew & Baker's Juvenile Circulating Library, Boston. *Catalogue of* . . . . Boston: Mayhew and Baker, 1860. 16 p. (Massachusetts Historical Society)

Mein's (John) Circulating Library, Boston. *Catalogue of* . . . . Boston: n.p., 1765. 57 p. (Massachusetts Historical Society)

Nash's (Melitiah?) Circulating Library, New York. *Explanatory Catalogue of* . . . . New York: Sage and Clough, 1803. 32 p. (New York Public Library)

New Circulating Library, Boston. *Catalogue of the* . . . . Boston: Munroe & Francis, 1804. 24 p. (American Antiquarian Society)

New Circulating Library, Boston. *Catalogue of Books in the* . . . . Boston: Charles Callendar, 1815. 57 p. (Boston Public Library)

Newburyport Circulating Library, Newburyport, Mass. *Catalogue of Books at the* . . . *, Kept at Charles Whipple's Book-store* . . . . [Newburyport, Mass.]: C. Norris & Co., 1816. 107 p. (American Antiquarian Society)

Peirce, Charles. *Catalogue of Books for Sale and Circulation* . . . . Portsmouth, N.H.: Charles Peirce, 1806. 103 p. (American Antiquarian Society)

Pelham's (William) Circulating Library, Boston. *Catalogue of* . . . . Charlestown, Mass.: Samuel Etheridge, 1801. 51 p. (American Antiquarian Society)

Pelham's (William) Circulating Library, Boston. *Catalogue of* . . . . Boston: Munroe & Francis, 1804. 62 p. (American Antiquarian Society)

Philadelphia Circulating Library. *Catalogue of the* . . . . Philadelphia: Thomas H. Palmer, 1824. 162 p. (Library Company of Philadelphia)

Philadelphia Circulating Library. *Supplement* [to the Catalogue of the . . .] n.p., 1828. (Library Company of Philadelphia)

Planters' Banner Circulating Library, Franklin, La. [Catalogue] In Franklin, La. *Planters' Banner*, April 8, July 15, August 26, October 7, 1847; January 6, July 28, 1848.

Portsmouth Book Store, Portsmouth, N.H. *Catalogue of Books, for Sale or Circulation, by Samuel Larkin, at the* . . . . Portsmouth: Samuel Larkin, 1796. 24 p. (American Antiquarian Society)

Roach's (J.) Circulating Library, Baltimore, Md. *Catalogue of* . . . . [Baltimore: n.p., 1826?] 104 p. (Maryland Historical Society)

Robinson's (Joseph) Circulating Library, Baltimore, Md. *Catalogue of* . . . . Baltimore: n.p., 1816. 154 p. (Enoch Pratt Free Library, Baltimore)

Robinson's (Joseph) Circulating Library, Baltimore, Md. *First Supplement for 1816, to the Catalogue of* . . . . Baltimore: n.p., 1816. 12 p. (Enoch Pratt Free Library, Baltimore)

Robinson's (Joseph) Circulating Library, Baltimore, Md. *Second Supplement, for 1817-1818, to the Catalogue of* . . . . Baltimore: J. Robinson, 1818. 12 p. (Maryland Historical Society)

Robinson's (Joseph) Circulating Library, Baltimore, Md. *Third Supplement, for 1819.* Baltimore: J. Robinson, 1819. 12 p. (Maryland Historical Society)

Robinson's (Martin) Circulating Library, Providence, R.I. *Catalogue of* . . . . Providence: John Miller, 1823. 52 p. (Brown University Library)

Robinson's (Martin) Circulating Library, Providence, R.I. *Catalogue of Additions* . . . , *from 1823 to January 1825.* n.p., n.d. 9 p. (Brown University Library)

Robinson's (Martin) Circulating Library, Providence, R.I. *Catalogue of Additions to . . . , from Jan. 1825 to Jan. 1827.* [Providence, R.I.?]: n.p., n.d. 6 p. (Brown University Library)

Robinson's (Martin) Circulating Library, Providence, R.I. *Additions to . . . for 1827.* [Providence?]: n.p., n.d. 7 p. (Brown University Library)

Robinson's (Martin) Circulating Library, Providence, R.I. *Additions to . . . , for 1829.* Providence: Eastman & Hall, n.d. 9 p. (Brown University Library)

Robinson's (Martin) Circulating Library, Providence, R.I. *Additions to . . . , for 1830 & 1831.* Providence: Cranston & Hammond, 1831. 16 p. (Brown University Library)

Saco Circulating Library, Saco, Me. *Catalogue of the Books Contained in the . . . , Kept by A. E. Small . . . .* Saco, Me.: W. J. Condon, 1834. 12 p. (Maine Historical Society)

Shakspeare Circulating Library, Boston. *Catalogue of the . . . .* Boston: Charles Callendar, 1819. 48 p. (Massachusetts Historical Society)

Shakspeare Circulating Library, Boston. *Catalogue of the . . . .* Boston: Charles Callendar, 1820. 48 p. (American Antiquarian Society) Same as 1819 catalogue above, but with new wrapper.

Streeter's (A.S. & G.M.) Circulating Library, Woonsocket Falls, R.I. "Catalogue of Books in . . . ." In Woonsocket *Patriot*, Nov. 16, 1833, 4: 4-7.

Tappan, Charles. *Catalogue of Books for Sale and Circulation . . . .* Portsmouth, N.H.: Stephen Sewall, 1809. 34 p. (American Antiquarian Society)

Union Circulating Library, Boston. *Catalogue of the . . . .* Boston: Munroe & Francis, 1806. 82 p. (American Antiquarian Society)

Union Circulating Library, Boston. *Catalogue of the . . . .* Boston: Samuel Avery, 1810. 80 p. (American Antiquarian Society)

Union Circulating Library, Boston. *Catalogue of the . . . .* [Boston]: S. H. Parker, 1812. 76 p. (Boston Public Library)

Union Circulating Library, Boston. *Catalogue of the* . . . . Boston: n.p., 1815. (American Antiquarian Society)

Union Circulating Library, Boston. *Catalogue of the* . . . . [Boston]: n.p., 1820. 128 p. (American Antiquarian Society)

Union Circulating Library, Philadelphia. *Catalogue of the* . . . . Philadelphia: Thomas H. Palmer, 1824. 102 p. (Library Company of Philadelphia)

Washington Circulating Library, Boston. *Catalogue of the* . . . . [Boston]: T. G. Bangs, 1817. 60, 12 p. (American Antiquarian Society)

Washington Circulating Library, Washington, Me. *Catalogue of Books Belonging to the . . . , Kept at the Bookstore of Pearson & Little* . . . . Portland: Day & Fraser, 1829. 23 p. (Detroit Public Library)

Waterville Circulating Library, Waterville, Me. [Catalogue] In *Waterville Intelligencer*, October 19, 26; November 2, 9, 1826.

Waverly Circulating Library, Waverly, Me. *Catalogue of the* . . . . Portland: James Adams, Jun., 1828. 12 p. (Detroit Public Library)

Subject Analysis of Circulating Library Catalogues

Percent of Holdings, By Subject

Library, Date	Approx. No. of Titles	Reference	Miscellany	Phil. Ethics	Theol. Rel.	Economics	Commerce	Govt. Poli.	Law	Science	Technology	Fine Arts	Rhetoric	Literature	Fiction	Geog. Travel	History	Biography
Mein, 1765	730	3	2	4	31	1		1	4	9	5		1	10	14	3	8	4
Aikman, 1773	820		4	7	2			2		1	2			24	25	7	20	7
Annapolis, 1783	720	1	1	3	6			1		6	4		1	13	42	5	13	9
Martin, 1786	525	2	3	5	7			2	2		7		4	10	35	8	4	6
Guild, 1788	550		2	8	7					3	1			22	31	8	7	9
Foster, Drown, 1789	150		7	12	9	1		3	1	6	3		3	22	15	4	23	2
Guild, 1789	970		1	10	6			1	4	3	8	1	1	7	34	9	8	6
Dabney, 1791	750		4	9	4			3	2	3	1			20	42	6	2	1
Guild (Add.) 1791	310		3	5	8		1	3	4	8	5	1	3	15	27	16	9	1
Blake, 1793	1,340	1		6	7		1	2	1	1	6	1	1	8	37	8	5	4
Dabney (Add.) 1794	790	1	3	13	7			3		4	4			14	26	8	8	8
Blake, 1796	1,485	2	1	5	9	1		2	4	6	3		1	7	50	5	8	3
Portsmouth, 1796	680	2	1	10	21	1		2	1	3	4	1	2	15	14	7	3	7
Blake, 1798	1,565	2	1	4	9			1	2	1	4		2	7	54	5	4	2
Caritat, 1799	2,995	1	5	4	5		1	4			2		2	28	30	4	6	6
Blake, 1800	900		3	4	1			3	1	1				11	63	7	3	5
Cushing, 1800	885			8	5			4				1		7	55	8	6	4
Dabney, 1801	1,770		5	13	3			1		1	1		1	14	41	7	7	7
Dietrick, 1801	905		4	11	11			4	1		4	3		13	33	3	6	7

Subject Analysis of Circulating Library Catalogues (continued)

Percent of Holdings, By Subject

Library, Date	Approx. No. of Titles	Reference	Miscellany	Phil. Ethics	Theol. Rel.	Economics	Commerce	Govt. Poli.	Law	Science	Technology	Fine Arts	Rhetoric	Literature	Fiction	Geog. Travel	History	Biography
Pelham, 1801	1,130		2	2	1			1	1	1				26	47	8	7	5
Berrian, 1803	1,070		2	6	10		1	4					1	19	33	9	6	8
Harwood, 1803	3,290		1	3	1		1	1	1					7	72	4	4	6
Nash, 1803	395	2	2	7	7			1		3	3		3	23	30	6	5	7
Caritat, 1804	3,150	2	6	7	1			2			3	1		21	41	5	7	6
New, 1804	590		1	6			1			1	1		1	19	48	10	3	8
Pelham, 1804	1,610			1	1							1		26	44	12	5	9
Peirce, 1806	2,215		2	9	20								1	8	22	4	3	4
Union, 1806	1,700		1	1					8	10	8			30	42	13	6	7
Baltimore, 1807	2,080		1					5						3	89	2	3	2
Baltimore (Add.) 1809	310			1				1			1			7	82			4
Tappan, 1809	945	1	1	5	20			1	12	9	3	2	2	24	5	9	2	4
Union, 1810	2,300		1	1	1			1						31	42	10	7	7
Baltimore, 1812	690	4		5	1			3	1	2	1		1	13	55	4	6	3
Union, 1812	1,445		4	3		1		1		2			1	16	67	1	1	3
Baltimore (Add.) 1813	100			3										4	88			4
Baltimore (Add.) 1814	535		7	2										6	84		1	1
New, 1815	1,145		3	2				2		2			1	15	46	10	8	10
Union, 1815	2,260		1	4				2		2			1	15	53	8	5	8
Newburyport, 1816	1,910		2	6	24			1		2	4		1	20	17	2	4	7

Percent of Holdings, By Subject

Library, Date	Approx. No. of Titles	Reference	Miscellany	Phil. Ethics	Theol. Rel.	Economics	Commerce	Govt. Poli.	Law	Science	Technology	Fine Arts	Rhetoric	Literature	Fiction	Geog. Travel	History	Biography
Ladies, 1829	2,320		2	2	1			1				1		18	62	3	4	7
Robinson (Add.) 1829	115			2						1				10	62	13	3	8
Washington, 1829	670		4	2	18				1		1			10	68	7	4	6
Coleman's Public, 1831	1,095		2	2	1			1		2	2		1	8	45	5	5	8
Robinson (Add.) 1831	270		2	1						1	1		1	8	49	14	10	12
Streeter, 1833	225		2	3	4					2	1			10	59	5	7	7
Coleman's Public, 1834	1,690	1	4	1	3				1	4	2			6	56	5	5	12
Franklin, 1834	800	1	4		2				1	2				10	52	13	5	8
Saco, 1834	280			3	2			1		4			1	7	42	11	12	18
Boylston, 1837	2,825		1	1	3									17	47	12	2	17
Coleman & Chisholm, 1837	957		1	1				1	1	1				4	71	4	12	4
Louisville, 1842	1,225			2	3			2	1	3	2			3	55	9	9	10
Planters' Banner, 1847	240														94	4		2
Loring, 1860	770				1			2		1		1		4	83	4	1	3
Mayhew & Baker, Central, 1860	875			1	1			1			1			3	81	2	1	9
Mayhew & Baker Juvenile, 1860	365			2							1				81	5	9	2
Cambridge, 1861	920		2	1				1		1					66	7	2	20
Campbell, 1870	1,605		1		5			1		1				1	85	3	3	1
Ellis, 1874	4,320			1	1			1						6	77	3	2	8
Kendrick, 188?	1,155		2		1	1									97			1
Baltimore, 1882	2,340		1	2	7			1			1			6	78	3	3	5
American, 1886	395			4						5		1		5	55	3	8	10

Bibliography

Alden, John E. "John Mein, Publisher: an Essay in Bibliographic Detection." *Papers of the Bibliographical Society of America* 36 (3d quarter 1942): 199-214.

Altick, Richard D. *The English Common Reader.* Chicago: University of Chicago Press, 1957.

Anderson, Edward P. "The Intellectual Life of Pittsburgh, 1786-1836." *Western Pennsylvania Historical Magazine* 14 (1931) 9-27, 92-114, 225-236, 288-309.

"Are Subscription Circulating Libraries Needed?" *Library Journal* 44 (December 1919): 778.

Baltimore American, July 20, 1809; May 30, 1812; November 1, 1822; September 18, 1822; April 15, 1823.

Baltimore Federal Gazette, October 13, 1804; September 5, 27, 1809; November 19, 1812; May 14, 1818.

Baltimore Gazette and Daily Advertiser, April 17, 1834.

Bibliotheca Americana; or A Chronological Catalogue of the Most Curious and Interesting Books, Pamphlets, State Papers, &c upon the Subject of North and South America. London: J. Debrett, 1789.

Blakey, Dorothy. *The Minerva Press, 1790-1820.* London: Bibliographical Society, 1939.

Blane, William. *Excursion through the United States and Canada.* London: Baldwin, 1824.

Bolton, Charles K. "Circulating Libraries in Boston, 1765-1865." *Publications of the Colonial Society of Massachusetts* 11 (February 1907): 196-207.

Boston Columbian Centinel, May 22, 1802; August 8, 1810; April 27, 1811; August 26, 1812; March 31, 1813; August 24, 1814; March 30, 1816; June 19, 1819.

Boston Gazette, October 7, 1765.

Boston Independent Chronicle, June 27, 1793; May 17, 1802; July 17, 1815; October 17, 1818.

Bowes, Frederick P. *The Culture of Early Charleston.* Chapel Hill: University of North Carolina Press, 1942.

Boyd, William D., Jr. "Books for Young Businessmen: Mercantile Libraries in the United States." Ph.D. dissertation, Indiana University, 1975.

Bradbury, John. *Travels in the Interior of America*. London: Sherwood, Neely, and Jones, 1819.

Bridenbaugh, Carl. "Press and Book in Eighteenth-Century Philadelphia." *Pennsylvania Magazine of History and Biography* 65 (January 1941): 1-30.

Bridenbaugh, Carl and Jessica. *Rebels and Gentlemen*. N.Y.: Reynal & Hitchcock, 1942.

Briggs, F. Allen. "The Sunday School Library in the Nineteenth Century." *Library Quarterly* 31 (April 1961): 166-77.

Brotherhead, William. *Forty Years among Old Booksellers of Philadelphia*. Philadelphia: A. P. Brotherhead, 1891.

Brown, H. Glenn and Maude O. *Directory of Printing, Publishing, Bookselling & Allied Trades in Rhode Island to 1865*. N.Y.: New York Public Library, 1958.

Brown, H. Glenn and Maude O. *Directory of the Book-Arts and Book Trade in Philadelphia to 1820*. N.Y.: New York Public Library, 1950.

Bullock, W. *Sketch of a Journey through the Western States of North America*. London: John Miller, 1827.

Callister, Henry. Family papers, ca. 1741-88. Maryland Historical Society.

Carey, Mathew. Letter books, 1809. Historical Society of Pennsylvania.

Carrier, Esther Jane. *Fiction in Public Libraries, 1876-1900*. N.Y.: Scarecrow, 1965.

Cazden, Robert E. "Libraries in the German-American Community and the Rise of the Public Library Movement." *Milestones to the Present; Papers from Library History Seminar V*, ed. by Harold Goldstein. Syracuse: Gaylord Professional Publications, 1978. pp. 193-211.

Cecil, Henry L. and Heaps, Willard A. *School Library Service in the United States*. N.Y.: H. W. Wilson, 1940.

Chicago Tribune, October 26, 1871.

Coe, Ellen M. "Fiction." *Report of the Commissioner of Education for the Year 1892-93*. Washington, D.C.: Government Printing Office, 1895. pp. 933-39.

Cohen, Hennig. *The South Carolina Gazette, 1732-1775.* Columbia: University of South Carolina Press, 1953.

Conklin, Groff. "Rental Libraries: Problems and Prospects —Part 1." *Publishers' Weekly* 165 (April 24, 1954): 1818-21.

Crumrine, Boyd, ed. *History of Washington County, Pennsylvania.* Philadelphia: L. H. Everts & Co., 1882.

Cuming, Fortescue. *Sketches of a Tour to the Western Country.* Pittsburgh: Cramer, Spear & Eichbaum, 1810.

Curless, Martha. "Library Development in LaGrange County, Indiana." *Contributions to Mid-West Library History,* ed. by Thelma Eaton. Champaign, Ill.: Illini Bookstore, 1964. pp. 164-80.

Dana, John Cotton. "Fiction in Libraries." *Current Literature* 33 (August 1902): 233-34.

Dana, John Cotton. *A Library Primer.* Chicago: Library Bureau, 1899.

Davis, John. *Travels of Four Years and a Half in the United States of America.* Bristol: E. Edwards, 1803.

Detroit Free Press, June 10, 1877.

Dewey, Melvil. "Libraries As Related to the Educational Work of the State." *Report of the Commissioner of Education for the Year 1887-88.* Washington, D.C.: Government Printing Office, 1889. pp. 1031-39.

Ditzion, Sidney. "The District-School Library, 1835-55." *Library Quarterly* 10 (October 1940): 545-77.

"Dull Times." *Publishers' Weekly* 12 (July 7, 1877): 6.

Dunn, Jacob Piatt. *Greater Indianapolis.* 2 vols. Chicago: Lewis, 1910.

Dunn, Jacob Piatt. *Libraries of Indiana.* Indianapolis: W. B. Burford, 1893.

Eaton, Thelma, ed. *Contributions to American Library History.* Champaign, Ill.: Illini Bookstore, 1961.

Ellis, Franklin and Evans, Samuel. *History of Lancaster County, Pennsylvania.* Philadelphia: Everts & Peck, 1883.

"Essays." *Boston Weekly Magazine* 1 (January 22, 1803): 53.

Evans, Charles. *American Bibliography*. 14 vols. N.Y.: P. Smith, 1941-1962.

"Fiction Song." *Library Journal* 15 (November 1890): 325.

Flener, Jane G. "A History of Libraries in Tennessee before the Civil War." Ph.D. dissertation, Indiana University, 1963.

Fletcher, Doris M. "Read a Book and Sin No More: The Early YMCA Libraries." *Wilson Library Bulletin* 31 (March 1957): 521-22.

Forrest, Earle R. *History of Washington County, Pennsylvania*. 3 vols. Chicago: S. J. Clarke, 1926.

Franklin, Benjamin. *Autobiography*. New Haven, Conn.: Yale University Press, 1964.

Georgia Gazette, January 26, 1798.

Goodrich, S. G. *Recollections of a Lifetime*. 2 vols. N.Y.: Miller, Orton and Mulligan, 1856.

Griest, Guinevere L. *Mudie's Circulating Library and the Victorian Novel*. Bloomington: Indiana University Press, 1970.

Growoll, Adolf. *Book Trade Bibliography in the United States in the Nineteenth Century*. N.Y.: Burt Franklin, 1939.

Hamilton, Alexander. *Gentleman's Progress: The Itinerarium of Dr. Alexander Hamilton, 1744*. Chapel Hill: University of North Carolina Press, 1948.

Hamilton, Milton W. *The Country Printer, New York State, 1785-1830*. N.Y.: Columbia University Press, 1936.

Hanson, Marcus Lee. *The Atlantic Migration, 1607-1860*. N.Y.: Harper, 1961.

Hatch, Orin W. *Lyceum to Library; A Chapter in the Cultural History of Houston*. Houston: Texas Gulf Coast Historical Association, 1965.

Held, Ray E. *Public Libraries in California, 1849-1878*. Berkeley: University of California Press, 1963.

Henry, W. E., comp. *Municipal and Institutional Libraries of Indiana*. n.p.: Louisiana Purchase Exposition Commission of Indiana, 1904.

Hoffman, Edwin D. "The Bookshops of New York City, 1743-1948." *New York History* 30 (January 1949): 53-65.

Hutchins, B. L. "Arkansas Enjoyed Libraries and Books Back in the 1840s." *Arkansas Libraries* 6 (October 1949): 11-12.

Indianapolis State Gazette, July 29, 1830.

Ithaca (N.Y.) *Journal*, June 15, 1825; May 3, 1826.

Jefferson, Thomas. *Writings*. 20 vols. Washington, D.C.: Thomas Jefferson Memorial Association, 1907.

Joeckel, Carleton B. *The Government of the American Public Library*. Chicago: University of Chicago Press, 1935.

Kaser, David. "Bernard Dornin, America's First Catholic Bookseller." *Books in America's Past*, ed. by David Kaser. Charlottesville: University Press of Virginia, 1966. pp. 105-28.

Kaser, David. "Coffee House to Stock Exchange: A Natural History of the Reading Room." *Milestones to the Present; Papers from Library History Seminar V*, ed. by Harold Goldstein. Syracuse: Gaylord Professional Publications, 1978. pp. 238-54.

Kaser, David. *Directory of the St. Louis Book and Printing Trades to 1850*. N.Y.: New York Public Library, 1961.

Kaser, David. *Joseph Charless, Printer in the Western Country*. Philadelphia: University of Pennsylvania Press, 1963.

Kaser, David. *Messrs. Carey & Lea of Philadelphia*. Philadelphia: University of Pennsylvania Press, 1957.

Kaser, David. "Waverley in America." *Papers of the Bibliographical Society of America* 51 (1957): 163-67.

Keep, Austin B. *History of the New York Society Library*. N.Y.: DeVinne Press, 1908.

Keller, Herbert A. "Solon Robinson." *Indiana Historical Collections*, Vol. XXI, No. 1, 1936.

Kelly, Thomas. *Early Public Libraries*. London: Library Association, 1966.

Kelly, Thomas. *A History of Public Libraries in Great Britain, 1845-1965*. London: Library Association, 1973.

Knauss, James Owen, Jr. *Social Conditions among the Pennsylvania Germans in the Eighteenth Century.* Lancaster: Pennsylvania-German Society, 1922.

Lamberton, E. V. "Colonial Libraries of Pennsylvania." *Pennsylvania Magazine of History and Biography* 42 (no. 3, 1918): 193-234.

Der Lancaster Correspondent, January 25, July 12, 1800.

Laugher, Charles T. *Thomas Bray's Grand Design.* Chicago: American Library Association, 1973.

Lehmann-Haupt, Hellmut. *The Book in America.* N.Y.: R. R. Bowker, 1939.

"Literary Intelligence." *Port Folio* 5 (September 7, 1805): 277.

Littlefield, George E. *Early Boston Booksellers, 1642-1711.* Boston: Club of Odd Volumes, 1900.

McCutcheon, Roger Philip. "Libraries in New Orleans, 1771-1833." *Louisiana Historical Quarterly* 20 (January 1937): 152-58.

McDermott, John Francis. "Public Libraries in St. Louis, 1811-1839." *Library Quarterly* 14 (January 1944): 9-27.

MacFarlane, John J. *History of Early Chestnut Hill.* Philadelphia: City History Society of Philadelphia, 1927.

McKay, George L. "A Register of Artists, Booksellers, Printers and Publishers in New York City, 1781-1800." *Bulletin of the New York Public Library* 45 (1941): 387-95; 483-99.

McKelvey, Blake, ed. *The History of Rochester Libraries.* Rochester, N.Y.: Rochester Historical Society, 1937.

McNeil, Gladys. "History of the Library in Arkansas." Thesis, University of Mississippi, 1957.

[Maestri, Helen] "New Orleans Public Library in the Nineteenth Century." *Louisiana Library Association Bulletin* 15 (Spring 1952): 35-43.

Martin, Dorothy V. "A History of the Library Movement in Ohio to 1850." Thesis, Ohio State University, 1935.

Maryland Gazette, September 2, 1762; January 13, February 10, 1763; April 5, 1764; July 1, November 11, 1773.

Maryland Journal and Baltimore Advertiser, October 23-30, 1773.

Massachusetts Gazette, October 31, 1765.

Maximilian, Prince of Wied. *Travels in the Interior of North America*. London: Ackerman, 1843.

Mease, James. *The Picture of Philadelphia*. Philadelphia: B. & T. Kite, 1811.

Melcher, Frederic G. "Should Popular Demand for Current Ephemeral Books Be Met by Rental Libraries? Yes!" *American Library Association Bulletin* 26 (September 1932): 707-09.

Miller, Samuel. *Brief Retrospect of the Eighteenth Century*. 2 vols. N.Y.: T. J. Swords, 1803.

Missouri Gazette, May 15, 1818.

Missouri Republican, January 1, July 23, 1833.

[Mitchell, John] *Reminiscences of Scenes and Characters in College*. New Haven, Conn.: A. H. Maltby, 1847.

Monaghan, Frank and Lowenthal, Marvin. *This Was New York, the Nation's Capital in 1789*. N.Y.: Doubleday, Doran, 1943.

Moore, Mary V. "Circulating Libraries in the Southeastern United States, 1762-1842." Thesis, University of North Carolina, 1958.

National Union Catalog; Pre-1956 Imprints.   vols. London: Mansell, 1968-   .

New Hampshire. State Librarian. *Report to the New Hampshire Legislature for the Year Ending October 1, 1891*. Concord, N.H.: n.p., 1891.

New Orleans Directory, 1830.

New-York Gazette, August 29, September 12, 1763.

New-York Gazette and Weekly Mercury, January 24, November 21, 1774.

New-York Journal, September 1, 1768.

New-York Packet, and the American Advertiser, January 4, 1776.

New Yorker, June 11, 1836.

Noble, A. D. "Short Survey of Libraries in the District of Columbia from the Beginning to the Civil War Period." *D. C. Libraries* 4 (April 1933): 70-87.

"Note." *Pennsylvania Magazine of History and Biography* 24 (no. 4, 1900): 526.

"Notes." *Library Journal* 14 (July 1889): 322.

"Novel Reading a Cause of Female Depravity." *Monthly Mirror* 4 (November 1797): 277-79.

Palmer-Poroner, Bruno J. "The Library Movement in Reading, 1820-1860." *Historical Review of Berks County* 7 (April 1942): 70-74.

Patrick, Walton R. "A Circulating Library of Ante-Bellum Louisiana." *Louisiana Historical Quarterly* 23 (January 1940): 131-40.

Pawtucket (R.I.) *Chronicle*, February 17, 1832.

Pennsylvania Chronicle, September 14, 1767; December 4, 1769; January 8, 1770.

Pennsylvania Gazette, January 12, 1769; January 3, 1771.

Pennsylvania Journal, September 21, 1769.

Pennsylvania Packet, December 23, 1771; March 14, 1774.

Perkins, Alice J. G. and Wolfson, Theresa. *Frances Wright: Free Enquirer*. N.Y.: Harper, 1939.

Philadelphia Aurora, December 8, 1797; May 30, 1798; January 1, November 4, 1799.

Pinner, H. L. *The World of Books in Classical Antiquity*. Leiden: Sijthoff, 1958.

Pittsburgh Gazette, July 26, 1788; April 11, 1789; January 30, 1790; December 22, 29, 1798.

Poste, Leslie I. "How the Library Came to Denver." *Westerners Brand Book* 5 (October 1948): 41-43.

"Present Rental Library Practice, Part II." *Publishers' Weekly* 132 (September 25, 1937): 1318-22.

Putnam, George H. *Books and Their Makers during the Middle Ages*. 2 vols. N.Y.: Hillary House, 1962.

Raddin, George Gates. *Caritat and the Genet Episode*. Dover, N.J.: Dover Advance Press, 1953.

Raddin, George Gates. *An Early New York Library of Fiction*. N.Y.: H. W. Wilson, 1940.

Raddin, George Gates. *Hocquet Caritat and the Early New York Literary Scene*. Dover, N.J.; Dover Advance Press, 1953.

Raddin, George Gates. *The New York of Hocquet Caritat and His Associates*. Dover, N.J.: Dover Advance Press, 1953.

Reichmann, Felix. "German Printing in Maryland; A Check List, 1768-1950." *Report of the Society for the History of the Germans in Maryland* 27 (1950): 9-70.

"Rental Libraries Public and Private." *Publishers' Weekly* 104 (August 18, 1923): 544-45.

"Rental Library Competition." *Publishers' Weekly* 104 (August 18, 1923): 541-42.

"Rental Library vs. Public Library." *Publishers' Weekly* 104 (August 11, 1923): 486.

Rhees, William J. *Manual of Public Libraries, Institutions, and Societies in the United States, and British Provinces in North America.* Philadelphia: J. B. Lippincott, 1859.

Richmond (Ind.) Palladium, Feb. 3, 1838.

Rivington's New-York Gazetteer, December 30, 1773.

"The Roving Library of Vesta Eales." *Publishers' Weekly* 138 (July 20, 1940): 162-63.

Rowson, Susanna, *Mentoria.* 2 vols. Philadelphia: Robert Campbell, 1794.

Royall, Anne Newport. *Mrs. Royall's Pennsylvania, or Travels Continued in the United States.* 2 vols. Washington, D.C.: The Author, 1829.

Sabine, Julia Elizabeth. "Antecedents of the Newark Public Library." Ph.D. dissertation, University of Chicago, 1947.

Salem (Mass.) Register, October 23, 1819.

Saucerman, Kathryn. "A Study of the Wisconsin Library Movement, 1850-1900." Thesis, University of Wisconsin, 1944.

Savannah Columbian Museum, April 26, 1799.

Scharf, J. and Westcott, Thompson. *History of Philadelphia, 1609-1884.* 3 vols. Philadelphia: L. H. Everts, 1884.

Sharp, Katharine L. *Illinois Libraries.* Urbana: University of Illinois, 1906-1908.

Shaw, Ralph R. *American Bibliography; A Preliminary Checklist for 1801-1819.* 22 vols. N.Y.: Scarecrow, 1958-1966.

Shera, Jesse H. *Foundations of the Public Library*. Chicago: University of Chicago Press, 1949.

Shoemaker, Richard H. *Checklist of American Imprints for 1820-* vols. N.Y.: Scarecrow, 1964-

Sills, R. Malcolm. " 'The Trumbull Manuscript Collections' and Early Connecticut Libraries." *Papers in Honor of Andrew Keogh, Librarian of Yale University.* New Haven, Conn.: Privately Printed, 1938. pp. 325-42.

Silver, Rollo G. *The Baltimore Book Trade, 1800-1825.* N.Y.: New York Public Library, 1953.

Silver, Rollo G. *The Boston Book Trade, 1800-1825.* N.Y.: New York Public Library, 1949.

Skallerup, Harry. *Books Afloat & Ashore.* Hamden, Conn.: Archon, 1974.

South Carolina Gazette, April 27, 1765; July 20, 1767; November 12, 1772.

Spencer, Gwladys. "The Chicago Public Library; Origins and Background." Ph.D. dissertation, University of Chicago, 1940.

Stern, Madeleine B. *Books and Book People in 19th-Century America.* N.Y.: R. R. Bowker, 1978.

Stern, Madeleine B. *Imprints on History.* Bloomington: Indiana University Press, 1956.

Stewart, Jeannette. "Library Service in Alaska, a Historical Survey." Thesis, University of Washington, 1957.

Stiffler, Stuart A. "The Antecedents of the Public Library in the Western Reserve, 1800-1860." Thesis, Western Reserve University, 1957.

Stone, Edwin M. *History of Beverly, Civil and Ecclesiastical, from Its Settlement in 1630 to 1842.* Boston: J. Munroe, 1843.

Stone, Elizabeth W. *American Library Development, 1600-1899.* N.Y.: H. W. Wilson, 1977.

Stuart, James. *Three Years in North America.* 2 vols. Edinburgh: Robert Cadell, 1833.

Sutton, Walter. *The Western Book Trade: Cincinnati as a Nineteenth-Century Publishing and Book-Trade Center.* Columbus: Ohio State University Press, 1961.

Tapley, Harriet S. *Salem Imprints, 1768-1825*. Salem, Mass.: The Essex Institute, 1927.

Tebbel, John. *History of Book Publishing in the United States*. 2 vols. N.Y.: R. R. Bowker, 1972-1975.

Thomas, Isaiah. *History of Printing in America*. N.Y.: Weathervane, 1970.

Thompson, C. Seymour. *Evolution of the American Public Library, 1653-1876*. Washington, D.C.: Scarecrow, 1952.

Ticknor, George. *Life, Letters, and Journals*. 2 vols. Boston: James R. Osgood & Co., 1876.

Tinker, Edward L. "Boimare, First and Still Foremost Bibliographer of Louisiana." *Papers of the Bibliographical Society of America* 24 (1930): 34-42.

Tolman, Frank L. "Libraries and Lyceums." New York State Historical Association, *History of the State of New York*. 10 vols. N.Y.: Columbia University Press, 1933-1937. 9: 45-91.

Town Topics 18 (September 15, 1887): 7.

Trollope, Frances. *Domestic Manners of the Americans*. N.Y.: Knopf, 1974.

U.S. Bureau of Education. *Catalog of "A.L.A. Library."* Washington, D.C.: Government Printing Office, 1893.

U.S. Bureau of Education. *Public Libraries in the United States of America . . . Special Report. Part I*. Washington, D.C.: Government Printing Office, 1876.

U.S. Bureau of Education. *Report . . . for the Year 1884-1885*. Washington, D.C.: Government Printing Office, 1886.

U.S. Bureau of the Census. *A Century of Population Growth*. Washington, D.C.: Government Printing Office, 1909.

Varma, Devendra P. *The Evergreen Tree of Diabolical Knowledge*. Washington, D.C.: Consortium Press, 1972.

Walter, Frank K. "A Poor but Respectable Relation; The Sunday-School Library." *Library Quarterly* 12 (July 1942): 731-39.

Warren (R.I.) *Clarion*, March 27, 1824.

Waterville (Me.) *Intelligencer*, October 19, 26, November 2, 9, 1826.

Wheeler, Joseph T. "Booksellers and Circulating Libraries in Colonial Maryland." *Maryland Historical Magazine* 34 (June 1939): 111-37.

Wood, Raymond F. "Public Libraries in California, 1850-1920." *Milestones to the Present; Papers from Library History Seminar V*, ed. by Harold Goldstein. Syracuse: Gaylord Professional Publications, 1978. pp. 155-65.

Woodruff, Edwin H. "Fiction in Public Libraries." *Library Journal* 20 (October 1895): 342-45.

Wright, J. E. and Corbett, Doris S. *Pioneer Life in Western Pennsylvania*. Pittsburgh: University of Pittsburgh Press, 1940.

Wright, Louis B. *Cultural Life of the American Colonies*. N.Y.: Harper & Row, 1957.

Wright, Louis B. *Culture on the Moving Frontier*. N.Y.: Harper, 1955.

Wright, Lyle H. *American Fiction, 1851-1875*. San Marino, Cal.: Huntington Library, 1965.

Wright, Lyle H. *American Fiction, 1876-1900*. San Marino, Cal.: Huntington Library, 1966.

Wright, Lyle H. "Statistical Survey of American Fiction, 1774-1850." *Huntington Library Quarterly* 2 (April 1939): 309-18.

Wroth, Lawrence C. *The Colonial Printer*. Charlottesville: University Press of Virginia, 1964.

Wroth, Lawrence C. *History of Printing in Colonial Maryland*. Baltimore: Typothetae, 1922.

Zimmerman, Johann Georg von. *Strictures on National Pride*. Philadelphia: Bell, 1778.

Index

(189)

Franklin Circulating Library, 168, 175-176

Gaine, Hugh, 27
Gifford, Samuel, 35, 40
Gilkison, John, 49
Godwin, William, *Caleb Williams, St. Leon,* 46
Goethe, Johann Wolfgang von, *Sorrows of Young Werther,* 46
Goodrich (A. T.) and Company, 168, 175
Grange, Joseph de la, 51
Great Awakening, 7
Green, Jonas, 19
Guild, Benjamin, 55, 79, 168, 173
Guy Rivers, by William Gilmore Simms, 65

Hammond, James, 97-99, 124
Harris, Benjamin, 11
Harris, Hannah, 69
Harwood's (John) Circulating Library, 168, 174
Hawkins' Circulating Library, 98
The Hawks of Hawk Hollow, by Robert Montgomery Bird, 65
Hermsprong, by Robert Bage, 46
History of England, by Thomas Babington Macaulay, 65
History of New York, by Washington Irving, 66
History of Scotland, by William Robertson, 65
History of the Discovery of America, by Henry Trumbull, 65
Holcroft, Thomas, *Anna St. Ives, Hugh Trevor,* 46
Horse Shoe Robinson, by John Pendleton Kennedy, 65
Hugh Trevor, by Thomas Holcroft, 46
Hunter, Lucy, 69
Hunter & Robinson, 119
Hütter, Christian Jacob, 51

Inchbald, Elizabeth, *Nature and Art, Simple Story,* 46
The Infidel, by Robert Montgomery Bird, 65
Irving, Washington, *Astoria, Conquest of Granada, History of New York,* 65-66

Jefferson, Thomas, 89-90; *Notes on the State of Virginia,* 45
Jemison, Mary, autobiography, 66
Jordan, Miss, 69

Kendrick's Circulating Library, 168, 176
Kennedy, John Pendleton, *Horse Shoe Robinson, Swallow Barn,* 65

Ladies Circulating Library, 68-69, 168, 176
Lahn, Jacob, 51
Lamb, George, 49-50
Lane, William, 57
Larkin, Samuel, 48-49
Lever, Charles, 65
Lewis, Matthew Gregory, *The Monk,* 46-47
Leypoldt, Frederick, 104
Librairie de la Famille, 98
Libraries, Circulating, aboard barges, packets, riverboats, 71; access by women, 68-71, 77-78; branches, 105-106, 122; chains, 106; early nineteenth century, 66-71; England, 14-15; Europe, 15; fiction, 94, 102-104, 118-120; foreign-speaking clienteles, 51-52, 98; home-delivery, 96, 108, 122; hours of service, 121-122; influence of, 121-125; initiatives, 116-122; longevity of, 101-102; mortality rate, 101-102; popular books, 118-120; prestige of, 124; reading rooms, 71-76, 120-122; size of,

THREE THOUSAND COPIES OF THIS BOOK
HAVE BEEN PRINTED ON 60 LB MOHAWK VELLUM
THE TEXT IS COMPOSED IN 10PT LINOTYPE BASKERVILLE
WITH DISPLAY IN 21PT CANCELLERESCA BASTARDA
SET UNDER THE SUPERVISION OF CARL HILLMAN
ON A FORMAT DESIGNED BY BRUCE CAMPBELL
COMPOSED AND PRINTED OFFSET BY
PRINCETON UNIVERSITY PRESS

· MCMLXXX ·